Turbulent Spinsters

Women's Fight
for the Vote in Hastings
and St Leonards

ANN KRAMER

For my sister, Jay

Circaidy Gregory Press

ISBN 978-1-910841-46-4

Printed in the UK
by Catford Print

Published by Circaidy Gregory Press
Creative Media Centre,
45 Robertson Street
Hastings, Sussex
TN34 1HL

www.circaidygregory.co.uk

Contents

INTRODUCTION

2018 MARKS 100 YEARS SINCE British women gained the parliamentary vote for the first time. It was a major landmark in women's long march for political rights and citizenship, enabling women not only to vote for who should represent them in parliament but also to put themselves forward for election.

The women's vote wasn't just handed to them. It was hard won. Women campaigned and fought for more than 50 years in a remarkable campaign that, as it gathered momentum, expanded to involve literally tens of thousands of women all over the country. Some of the big, dramatic events such as the women's Mud March, or the rushes on the Houses of Parliament, are iconic events that are reasonably well known. Also well known are some of the charismatic personalities, among them the Pankhursts or Emily Davison, whose funeral march after she was killed by the King's horse on Derby day stopped crowds as it wound its way through London streets.

But this glorious campaign did not just take place in the big metropolitan cities such as London, Leeds or Manchester. It took place in towns and villages all over Britain, including Hastings and St Leonards. I am a Londoner but have lived in Hastings since the early 1970s. It's been my home for more than 40 years and with the centenary approaching, I was keen to find out what happened here, in Hastings and St Leonards. I wanted to find out how much women here contributed to the Cause, as the campaign for the woman's vote was known.

This meant poring over the archived – and happily for me, digitised – copies of the *Hastings and St Leonards Observer*, from the late 1860s and the beginning of the campaign through to the outbreak of the First World War and the achievement of the vote in 1918. The newspapers were a fantastic resource: in those far off days before radio and television – before mobile phones with their recording and camera facilities were even imaginable – it was the local newspaper that listed events and provided the intricate detail that is so fascinating for the researcher.

My research journey uncovered a thriving, articulate and very active local women's suffrage campaign in which determined women threw open their homes, particularly their drawing rooms, for suffrage meetings, booked public venues, invited speakers, shot off letters to the local paper, marched, protested, demonstrated, sold suffrage papers, made cups of tea, decorated meeting halls and in so many ways dedicated themselves and put their energies into achieving what they knew was their right – the vote.

It was fascinating to encounter names and personalities, many of whom I had never heard of before, holding meetings and public events in the roads, on the seafront and in the squares of the town that I live in and have walked through. Wellington Square, Warrior Square, Norman Road, Pelham Crescent, Eversfield Place and many other local places were sites of marches or meetings, or venues for invited speakers including Emmeline and Christabel Pankhurst, very big names in the campaign.

The remarkable suffrage campaign in Hastings and St Leonards filled the newspapers and engaged many women – married, unmarried, widows, teachers, doctors, actors and landed gentry. In many ways, and this is perhaps the joy of local history, the campaign in Hastings and St Leonards provides a microcosm of the wider campaign taking place across the country and even in other countries. The big political issues, the arguments, the set backs, the frustrations and the battles that were being lived, debated and confronted on the bigger stage, were also taking place on a smaller stage down here. Focusing in on the Hastings and St Leonards suffrage campaign provides a greater insight into how women were campaigning in their daily lives and within their own community.

I should not have been surprised to discover that women were so active locally because Hastings consistently seems to have produced or attracted a fair number of radical individuals. Barbara Bodichon, probably one of the most significant figures in the early women's movement was born locally and grew up here, so too did medical pioneer Sophia Jex-Blake. Hastings seafront was not only the venue for suffrage meetings but also fiery socialist gatherings. And this radical activism continues today with individual women involved in myriad campaigns and political meetings in the town centre demanding greater social justice, an end to austerity and challenging inequalities across the board.

I hope this personally rewarding research makes a useful contribution to the 2018 celebrations of a great achievement by women. Women's fight for the vote was perhaps one of the most significant, creative and inspiring of all political campaigns. But 1918 was only a start. It would be another ten years before women had voting rights equal with men and many more years before equality legislation was introduced. Thanks to women being in the political arena, there have been improvements and greater rights. However, one hundred years later women still have barriers to cross and sexism to challenge. Hastings is full of radical women; I have no doubt they will continue to fight for women's rights.

I would like to thank Kay Green for her sensitive editing and for agreeing to publish my book; I am grateful for her help and support. My thanks also to Erica Smith for her design expertise and to Emily Johns for creating a glorious front cover. Acknowledgements to The Keep, the Museum of London, Mary Evans Picture Library and Phasewire / Richard Pollard for permission to reproduce images and thanks to the Muriel Matters Society for their help.

CHAPTER 1

Early beginnings

'The Suffragettes have visited Hastings and left their mark!'

Shock and outrage swept through Hastings and St Leonards when, in the early hours of 15 April 1913, suffragettes set fire to the local Tory MP's former house Levetleigh, a rather stately mansion in St Leonards. Fortunately the house was empty and no one was hurt though the house itself was seriously damaged. Hardly surprisingly the event brought Hastings directly into the national press: both the *Hastings Observer* and *The Times* described the arson attack as a 'suffragist outrage' and launched a scathing attack not only on those directly responsible but also on the level of militancy existing within the women's suffrage movement. This local event was not unique: just a few weeks later, in an attempt to publicise the cause of votes for women, suffragette Emily Davison ran out onto the racetrack at the

Levetleigh burns, April 1913   *Picture courtesy richardpollard.co.uk*

Epsom Derby, only to be trampled to death by the king's horse, while in March 1914 militant activist Mary Richardson horrified public opinion by taking an axe to Velazquez's *Rokeby Venus* in London's National Gallery.

Events such as these caused massive public outrage and may well have damaged support for the women's cause, although there was some sympathy for Emily Davison's tragic death. But these incidents and the accompanying militancy were significant as they marked a high point of rage and frustration for women who had been campaigning tirelessly, whether peacefully or militantly, for more than half a century to win the right to a parliamentary vote. Even those within the movement who deplored the militancy, recognized the frustration and anger women were feeling.

'Who made man the exclusive judge, if woman partake with him the gift of reason?'

Mary Wollstonecraft

Small beginnings

Many people see the dramatic activism of the early 20th century as the start of women's campaign for the vote but the first calls for a woman's right to vote had taken place more than 80 years earlier. The women's suffrage movement was well established and had been campaigning for many years by the time stately Levetleigh went up in flames.

The beginnings of any movement are always hard to pin down precisely and that is as true of the women's movement as of any other. In 1792 Mary Wollstonecraft, influenced by the calls for freedom and equality of the French Revolution, published *A Vindication of the Rights of Women*. In this she made the radical claim that if women shared with men the gift of reason they should be treated equally, a view that at the time led to her being described by the press as a 'hyena in petticoats'. Wollstonecraft was not the first woman to call for women's rights, and she did not call for the vote, but her feminist views were hugely influential and had a powerful impact on activists and feminists who followed her.

At this stage in Britain the right to vote was extremely limited: voting rights for women did not exist and the male vote was confined to the landowning classes, aristocrats and wealthy landowners – a mere three per cent of the population. Many of the large new industrial cities had no members of parliament. The newly emerging industrial middle classes were not represented in Parliament, let alone any of members of the working class, whether male or female. From the early 1800s therefore, and in the wake of the social upheavals of the Industrial Revolution, increasing numbers of people began to demand the reform of Parliament.

From the beginning women were involved in the movements for reform, even though the emphasis was primarily on men gaining the vote. In 1818 a Female Reform Society was formed in Lancashire and women were among the victims of the so-called Peterloo Massacre in 1819 when government cavalry troops charged a peaceful meeting of reform supporters at St Peter's Fields, Manchester. Eleven people were killed and 400 men, women, and children were injured.

During the 1820s, the Owenite or Utopian socialists, who included social reformer Robert Owen, recognized that rights for women were fundamental to their utopian socialist philosophy, a view of a society based on co-operation and mutual help rather than competition and self-interest. In 1825 Owenite socialist William Thompson published *An Appeal of One Half of the Human Race, Women, against the pretentions of the other Half, Men.* It was a scathing attack on male control over women and an important political work, which directly called for women to have 'the possession of equal political rights.' Interestingly, the *Appeal* was partly aimed at Liberal philosopher John Stuart Mill, who at the time was arguing that women did not need political rights because their fathers and husbands would represent them adequately. The book carried Thompson's name as author but was dedicated to Anna Wheeler, feminist, writer and staunch advocate for women's rights, who was probably chiefly responsible for its views. Wheeler was very active in the Owenite socialist movement, which at its height attracted a considerable number of working- and middle-class women.

In 1832 after considerable social agitation and protest, the First Reform Act was introduced. This enabled male householders to have the parliamentary vote, so effectively enfranchising a large number of middle-class men. Significantly, it was this first major piece of parliamentary reform that effectively established the idea of an exclusively male vote because it explicitly restricted the vote to 'male persons', a point that campaigners would return to.

That same year the maverick MP for Preston, Henry 'Orator' Hunt, presented the first woman's suffrage petition to the House of Commons. Hunt had for years been agitating for parliamentary reform and had been imprisoned for taking part in the mass meeting held on St Peter's Fields, Manchester in 1819. As the first petition to the House of Commons calling for women's suffrage, this was a landmark. The petitioner was Mary Smith, a ratepayer who argued that as she paid taxes, she should have a share in the election of parliamentary representatives, one of the arguments that would be used constantly in the years to come. The event is recorded in *Hansard* (3 August 1832 vol 14 c1086):

> *'Mr Hunt said he had a petition to present which might be a subject of mirth to some hon. Gentlemen, but which was one deserving of consideration. It came from a lady of rank and*

fortune – Mary Smith, of Stanmore, in the county of York.
The petitioner stated that she paid taxes, and therefore did
not see why she should not have a share in the election of a
Representative; she also stated that women were liable to all
the punishments of the law, not excepting death, and ought to
have a voice in the making of them; but so far from this, even
upon their trials, both judges and jurors were all of the opposite
sex. She could see no good reason for the exclusion of women
from social rights, while the highest office of the State, that of
the Crown, was open to the inheritance of females, and, as we
understood, the petition expressed her indignation against those
vile wretches who would not marry, and yet would exclude
females from a share in legislation. The prayer of the petition
was, that every unmarried female, possessing the necessary
pecuniary qualification, should be entitled to vote for Members
of Parliament.'

It is not recorded whether honourable members did fall about laughing at what was then an unusual demand but a response from Sir Frederick Trench, who said that he felt it would be 'rather awkward if a jury half males and half females were locked up together for a night... might lead to rather queer predicaments' suggests that honourable members did not take this petition seriously and indeed, according to Hansard, it was 'laid on the table', that is, shelved.

Even so women's demand for the suffrage, or vote, was now in the public arena and slowly the calls began to multiply, though initially as individual voices. During the late1830s and 1840s Chartism emerged – a largely working-class movement, disappointed by the narrow remit of the First Reform Bill. Thousands of working class people joined the movement, which focused on a series of demands expressed through the Great Charter. The Chartists wanted a radical reform of parliament; their demands included a secret ballot, equal electoral districts, annual parliaments and above all votes for all men – and women – over the age of 21. Subsequent Charters or petitions dropped the demand for the woman's vote to concentrate primarily on men but even so it has been estimated that women formed at least 80 of their own Chartist associations between 1837 and 1844.

Chartist women marched, attended rallies and lobbied Parliament and in 1840, even though by now the movement had officially dropped demands for votes for women, an imprisoned Chartist, RJ Richardson wrote to one Miss Mary Ann Moon, who lived in Perth, encouraging her to carry on 'fearlessly advocating the right of women to interfere in the affairs of state' and stating that her countrywomen had a duty to do so because '... bad laws will never cease to be, nor wicked legislators cease to rule, until every man of twenty-one years of age, and every woman of twenty, obtain, by their extraneous exertions a voice in the election of those whom reason and honesty qualify for law-makers and administrators.' Writing from his prison cell, RJ Richardson could not have known how long this was going to take.

Another woman calling for rights was Anne Knight. A Quaker, she had gained considerable political experience in the struggle against slavery. In 1840 she attended the World Anti-Slavery Convention, held at Exeter Hall in London, where she met American feminists Elizabeth Cady Stanton and Lucretia Mott, who were also delegates to the Convention. Women in that movement were beginning to draw parallels between their oppression as women and that of slaves; they also felt dismissed by male delegates to the Convention. Their concerns inspired them to campaign for equality for women. Knight had been involved in Chartism but was infuriated that they had dropped calls for women's suffrage. She criticised the movement for claiming that 'the class struggle took precedence over than for women's rights'. Knight challenged the Chartists, writing 'can a man be free, if a woman be a slave' and in 1850 wrote to the *Brighton Herald* demanding that Chartists should be campaigning for what she described as 'true universal suffrage'.

In 1851 an important essay was published in the *Westminster Review*, namely 'The Enfranchisement of Women'. It begins with the words: 'That women have as good a claim as men have, in point of personal right, to the suffrage…it would be difficult for anyone to deny.' The writer was Harriet Taylor, a philosopher and women's rights advocate, who by this time had married philosopher John Stuart Mill and had been influential in converting him to the cause of women's suffrage, a cause to which he would give enormous support, his best known published advocacy of women's rights appearing in *The Subjection of Women* in 1869.

Hastings' trailblazer

By the 1850s a number of women were coming together to campaign for greater rights and opportunities for women, so laying the basis of the first British women's rights movement. One of the most prominent of these women was Barbara Leigh Smith (later Bodichon), who lived in Hastings and was to have a great influence on the form and direction of the early women's suffrage movement.

Born in Whatlington, near Battle, Barbara Leigh Smith grew up in Hastings, living at 9 Pelham Crescent, one of the fine Regency buildings adjacent to St Mary's in the Castle. Described by political activist and writer Ray Strachey as 'tall, handsome, [and] generous', she was a remarkable powerhouse, who made a strong impression on all those who met her and who worked tirelessly for women's rights, ultimately playing a leading role in the creation of the women's suffrage movement. Today, thanks to local historian Helena Wojtczak, there is a commemorative blue plaque in Pelham Crescent.

Barbara Leigh Smith was born into a wealthy, radical and quite unusual family. Her paternal grandfather had been involved in the anti-slavery movement and her father, Benjamin Leigh Smith, MP for Norwich and a Hastings magistrate, was an enlightened and radical individual, who knew many of the leading radicals and thinkers of the day. Her parents never married, something that shocked her first cousin Florence Nightingale. Her mother died when she was young, leaving her father and a succession of housekeepers to bring up the household. Her father, believing that girls should have the same opportunities as boys, provided Barbara with a good education and, perhaps even more significantly, when she reached the age of 21, presented her with investments that brought her an annual income of £300. This gave Barbara an independence and freedom that was highly unusual for young women of the time.

Barbara's initial ambition was to be an artist, and by 1849 she was studying art at the newly opened Bedford Ladies College in London. She was part of a circle that included William Morris, Lizzie Siddal and she became close friends with writer George Elliot. Her closest friend was the poet and feminist, Bessie Rayner Parkes, whose family had come to live with them at Pelham Crescent. Together the two women strode around Hastings, painting and discussing the events of the day; they also went on a walking tour through Belgium, Germany and Austria. Barbara was friendly with many women artists, helping to set up the Society for Female Artists and petitioning the Royal Academy to accept women artists.

Perhaps because of her unusual independence, Barbara Leigh Smith was acutely aware of the disadvantages suffered by women and soon began to devote her time and energy to working for women's rights. She started putting her views into print, publishing various articles on the education of women in the *Hastings and St Leonards News* in 1848, under a pseudonym. She would continue to fire out articles for many years to come.

Barbara Leigh Smith continued painting for most of her life but she owes her place in history to her energetic commitment to women's rights, a cause to which she dedicated the majority of her time and energy. The newly opened railway line enabled her to travel easily between Hastings and London, where most of her political activity took place. Her first major political step was to expose the discriminatory nature of English law, particularly in relation to property. At that time in the words of Sir William Blackstone: 'husband and wife are one and that is he'. Married women had virtually no legal status. Amassing the evidence, in 1854 she published *A Brief Summary in Plain Language of the Most Important Laws Concerning Women*, an immensely influential pamphlet that, together with a back-up petition containing no less than 26,000 signatures, was placed in front of the Law Amendment Society and the House of Commons, setting in motion the processes that eventually led to the Married Women's Property Act of 1882.

'By marriage the very being or legal existence of a woman is suspended, or at least it is incorporated … into that of her husband, under whose wing, protection and cover she performs everything.'

William Blackstone, Commentary on the Laws of England, 1765

In 1859 Barbara Leigh Smith, who by now had married a French doctor, Eugene Bodichon, was working with other leading feminists of the day such as Jessie Boucherett and poet and philanthropist Adelaide Anne Proctor, to set up the Society for the Promotion of Employment for Women, in Langham Place, London. From here the 'ladies of Langham Place', as they were known, worked to open up employment opportunities for single women, such as printing, bookkeeping and shop work and setting up the first business school for girls. In 1857 she produced another pamphlet *Women and Work*, in which, echoing Mary Wollstonecraft's views, she made a scathing attack on the idea that women only existed for men's amusement and argued that a married woman's dependence on her husband was degrading. What women needed was well-paid work, equal opportunities and proper training. Together with Bessie Rayner Parkes, Barbara took over a genteel newspaper *The Englishwoman's Journal* and turned it into a campaigning mouthpiece, firing out articles and providing a forum for discussing women's politics and women's rights. Given the prevailing attitudes of the time, the British press was not sympathetic, frequently pouring scorn on Barbara Bodichon and her colleagues. Critics of these outspoken and pioneering women advised them to stay home and 'hold their tongues in a dignified manner.' Not surprisingly this had little impact on Barbara Bodichon who continued her pioneering political campaigning undeterred.

The Kensington Society

The inexhaustible Barbara Bodichon then turned her attention to votes for women, or the suffrage as it was most usually described, believing, as many other women activists were coming to believe, that without the vote women would make little progress in their fight for equality. In March 1865 she, together with other women, founded the Kensington Society, a forum where like-minded women could meet and debate various issues. Ray Strachey described it as Britain's 'first feminist committee' and indeed the founder members included not just Barbara Bodichon but also pioneering activists such as Emily Davies, the Misses Buss and Beale, Jessie Boucherett, Helen Taylor and Elizabeth Garrett Anderson, most of whom were fighting to open up higher education for women.

Soon however, the members began to focus on opening up the suffrage for women. A second reform bill proposing to extend the franchise to urban working class men was in the offing. The Conservative MP Benjamin Disraeli had made a speech to the House of Commons stating that if a woman, Queen Victoria, could govern the country, and if women could hold property, he could see no reason why they should not vote. Encouraged by these words, on 28 April 1866 Barbara Bodichon, Emily Davies and Jessie Boucherett drafted a petition to be presented to Parliament, which called for the enfranchisement of 'all householders, without distinction of sex, who possess property or rental qualifications as your Honourable House may determine.' The wording and pitch were clever: firstly, given the First Reform Bill, the petition recognized the need for property ownership and secondly, and more significantly, focused on enfranchising propertied single women. It excluded married women, not least because at this stage they had no rights over property; this right still sat with their husbands. In the years to come the question of whether married women should have the vote was to be a significant issue.

*'Give some women votes, and it will tend to make all women think seriously of all the concerns of the nation at large …
There is no reason why women should not take an interest in all the social questions… which occupy Parliament.'*

Barbara Bodichon, Reasons for and Against the Enfranchisement of Women, 1866

With no say in parliament, these early suffragists had to rely on sympathetic MPs, often known as 'friends in the House'. One of their most sympathetic parliamentarians was John Stuart Mill, by then Liberal MP for Westminster. Another was Henry Fawcett, later to marry Millicent Garrett Anderson, who would go on to lead the largest women's suffrage organisation in Britain. Both men were absolutely committed to women's rights.

Barbara Bodichon and her colleagues circulated their petition, gathering nearly 1500 signatures within just two weeks, including those of Florence Nightingale and Harriet Martineau, feminist, writer and social reformer, and in due course took it to down to the House of Commons. Barbara Bodichon was not well that day so Emily Davies and Elizabeth Garrett took the cumbersome document to the House of Commons. Being rather nervous, they hid the petition under a fruiterer's cart outside until Mill arrived and picked up the document, which he felt gave him sufficient ammunition to argue his case.

On 20 May 1867 during a debate on the Second Reform Bill, JS Mill presented the women's petition to the House of Commons and proposed an amendment to the Bill, which would give women equal political rights to men, suggesting that the word 'man' in the Bill should be replaced by the non-gender specific word 'people'. Mill made a long and stirring speech putting the case for suitably qualified women to be given the vote, saying among other things: 'Can it be pretended that women who manage an estate or conduct a business – who pay rates and taxes, often to a large amount, and frequently from their own earnings – many of whom are responsible heads of families and some of whom, in the capacity of schoolmistresses, teach much more than a great number of the male electors have ever learnt – are not capable of a function of which every male householder is capable?' The House of Commons was packed, many MPs having given up other engagements to be there to hear the subject debated, so unusual was it for the question of women voting to come before the House. However, despite JS Mill's stirring oratory the amendment was defeated by 196 votes to 73. It was, though, a very influential speech that converted some anti-suffragist members to the cause, notably Mr John Bright, who was one of the MPs who voted in favour. His brother, Jacob Bright, would go on to present another women's suffrage Bill in 1870.

The defeat was probably not surprising, given prevailing views of the time, which were illustrated by a scathing editorial in the *Hastings and St Leonards Observer* which on 5 March 1867 had lammed into the Radical press saying that it was 'hardly possible to write with sufficient gravity, and an avoidance of the keen sense of the ridiculous we feel when we contemplate the flounderings of the Radical press, which at one moment is driven to apologise for the vampant revilings of John Bright [radical MP for Birmingham], at another to indite in awful verboseness... the praises of Mill... whose latest idea is the philosophy of government by the gentler sex.' Clearly an unthinkable state of affairs for the editors of the local newspaper, and no doubt those of other national and local newspapers.

The Second Reform Bill became law in August 1867, by which time Benjamin Disraeli had become prime minister. The new Act gave the vote to around 1,500,000 men, male adult urban householders or leaseholders. There was nothing at all for women, despite Disraeli's apparently supportive words just a few months earlier.

Barbara Bodichon and her colleagues in the Kensington Society were naturally disappointed but they had established the bedrock of a women's suffrage movement that would grow to reach every corner of the British Isles, become a daily talking point in virtually every home and

> '*I think the most important thing is to make a demand and commence the first humble beginnings of an agitation.*'
>
> **Helen Taylor writing to Barbara Bodichon, May 1866**

workplace and would go on to be one of the most extraordinary and determined of all the political campaigns in British history.

In 1867 the Kensington Society transformed into the London Society for Women's Suffrage (LSWS); John Stuart Mill was invited to be president while other members included the indefatigable Barbara Bodichon, Helen Taylor, Frances Power Cobbe, Jesse Boucherett, Emily Davies, the Misses Buss and Beale and the young Millicent Garrett or Fawcett as she would become better known. Another member was Lydia Becker, a Mancunian, who in 1866 was inspired by a speech given by

Barbara Bodichon and converted to 'the cause'. She combined forces with Emily Davies and Elizabeth Wolstenholme to form the Manchester Women's Suffrage Committee, a very influential organisation. Lydia Becker went on to become a major driving force and helped to co-ordinate the women's suffrage movement nationally for some years.

Despite the defeat of 1867, these trailblazing activists were not downhearted. They intensified their efforts and the cause of votes for women began to spread as other women's suffrage societies began to spring up around Britain.

An interesting test case

In 1867 an interesting test case took place in Manchester. Lydia Becker of the Manchester Women's Suffrage Society discovered that Lilly Maxwell, a shop owner in Manchester had managed to slip her name on to the electoral register and had voted for Jacob Bright in the 1867 election. Lydia Becker set to and encouraged another 5,346 women householders to demand that they be registered to vote. The case (Chorlton v Lings) came before the Court of Common Pleas in November 1868 and was argued for by Richard Pankhurst, who would later marry Emmeline Pankhurst, and Sir John Coleridge. It was rejected, the court ruling that women could not vote in British elections.

CHAPTER 2

Meetings, meetings, meetings

'Perhaps it is that the ladies of Hastings are not yet ripe
for the ladies' franchise'

By the early 1870s, there were women's suffrage societies in London, Manchester, the West Country, Scotland and Ireland. The campaign to achieve the parliamentary vote was slowly gathering momentum, boosted by the fact that under the Municipal Franchise Act of 1869, women ratepayers had gained the right to vote in municipal or local elections. This slightly surprising development had come about largely through the efforts of Jacob Bright MP for Manchester, supported by Lydia Becker.

The question of whether women should have the parliamentary vote was by now gaining interest and being debated around the country, including in the seaside town of Hastings, described by one correspondent to the *Hastings and St Leonards Observer* as this 'fashionable watering place'. By and large the call was for single, property owning or rate paying women to be given the parliamentary vote. There were very few voices as yet calling for all women to have the vote.

It is not surprising there was local interest. Then as now, Hastings and its sister town St Leonards seem to have either produced or attracted a significant number of radical thinkers and political activists, including strong-minded women. As well as Barbara Bodichon, Hastings was home to other pioneers of the women's rights movement such as Sophia Jex-Blake, who was instrumental in opening up medical training for women and Elizabeth Blackwell, pioneering woman doctor who moved to the town in 1879. Also resident in the town were Emma Fricker-Hall, Mrs Darent Harrison, Mrs Colonel

Tubbs, and many others whose names are not known today, but who consistently hosted and attended women's suffrage meetings over the next several years, their names featuring in the local press as they bombarded the correspondence columns with letters in support of the cause. For some years these women would be high-profile activists in the vanguard of the local women's suffrage campaign. It was not a step to be taken lightly. Public opinion expected late Victorian women, particularly those of the middle-classes, to remain quietly in the private sphere of home; it was not considered appropriate for them to enter the public arena of politics.

The area's demography was also significant. By the late 19th century, women outnumbered men locally. In 1871 a census report showed that women made up 58 per cent of the local population, men 42 per cent, a situation that continued right up to the First World War. While the area, then as now, included many impoverished women struggling to survive as domestic workers, homeworkers or other low-paid trades, it was also an area where single women ran businesses such as guesthouses, or millinery. The newly developed area of St Leonards in particular attracted a number of independent, single businesswomen. As a result, votes for women was on the local public agenda and from the early 1870s, the weekly *Hastings and St Leonards Observer* consistently included articles on or comments about women's suffrage activity, its coverage increasing as the years went on.

Initially the local paper reported only on women's suffrage activity elsewhere. One of the earliest references was on 23 February 1870 when the *Hastings Observer* noted that a public meeting had taken place in Crewe at which Miss Lydia Becker had spoken in support of a bill being presented to the House of Commons by Mr Jacob Bright, MP. Bright had effectively taken over from Mill, who had lost his Westminster seat, and was one of the key 'friends in the House', leading the parliamentary campaign to support women. His bill was, however, lost in committee, setting a pattern that continued for some years. At this stage the women's suffrage movement focused on drawing up petitions for friendly MPs, who would then put forward private members bills. Every year from 1871 to 1883 bills for women's suffrage were introduced into parliament but were lost each time.

In the year 1870, the first time that women voted in local elections, Hastings and St Leonards had some 460 women ratepayers registered on the electoral roll for municipal elections, although apparently, and according to the *Hastings Observer*, only '75 ladies exercised their privilege', a rather low turnout which local opponents of votes for women used as ammunition to prove that women did not want the vote.

Women's suffrage comes to Hastings

The first women's suffrage meeting in Hastings took place on 27 April 1871, when Mrs Ronninger arrived in the town to give a talk on votes for women in the Castle Assembly Room. It was a novelty to see a woman speaking in public and the venue was packed as a large audience arrived to see her and hear what she was going to say. Public speaking was a new experience for most of the early suffragists and could be daunting: it took courage and determination but within a relatively short space of time, increasing numbers of women campaigners developed the necessary confidence, skills and experience, emerging as formidable public speakers and travelling all round the country promoting votes for women.

Already a confident and experienced speaker, Mrs Jane Ronninger, who subsequently spoke on women's rights in Dover, Snargate and other places in the south east, gave what the *Hastings Observer* described as 'a long but... highly interesting discussion of the claims of ladies to participate in the Parliamentary Franchise.' She started her talk by commenting that women who dared to claim their rights were often 'subjected to persecution or social ostracism' and went on to talk about the types of objections that were put forward whenever the women's vote was raised: that 'women had not intellect enough to vote', that they were not educated in the 'proper' use of the vote, and that interference in the political arena 'would rob women of much of their charm'. And indeed these were certainly among the most common objections put forward whenever votes for women was mentioned. They reflected prevailing views of the time and particularly the belief that men and women should inhabit different social spheres. Other anti-suffrage arguments included the belief that men were naturally leaders, more physically and intellectually capable of dealing with the hurly and burly of political life and national decision making; that women were intellectually and physically inferior; that women would lose their femininity if they gained the vote; and that anyway men were quite capable of representing women. As time went on anti-suffrage arguments became slightly more sophisticated but by and large they remained much the same, although with a later addition that if women voted, they would be bound to vote Tory, something that naturally concerned Liberal MPs.

Anticipating this argument, Mrs Ronninger said she believed that 'the woman's question', a term frequently used to describe women's rights, should not be a political party matter and that it should remain outside party politics, something on which suffragists differed, though at this stage most would have agreed. She did though comment that it was a 'singular fact' that those who most opposed women's rights were generally 'strong Tories, or men holding Conservative principles'.

Having cited examples of women who had proved themselves intellectually, such as Elizabeth Blackwell, the pioneering woman physician, the first qualified woman doctor to register in Britain, the acclaimed artist Rosa Bonheur, and Queen Elizabeth I, Mrs Ronninger challenged what she described as a male law and asked her audience whether educated women such as those she had mentioned were to be denied the vote in favour of less educated men. All women were asking for, she said, was 'a clear stage and no favour' to have a say in the making of laws that affected them. Women wanted the same right in parliamentary elections that they now had in local elections. Madame Ronninger explained that the request was for 'women who paid rent and taxes, were heads of families, and performed all the right and duties of citizens'. She finished by saying it was anomalous that however highly educated a woman might be, however much of her life was spent in doing good, however great a stake she had in the country, 'she was not deemed fit to be entrusted with the vote'. Following the talk a petition in favour of women's suffrage was circulated.

The issues that Mrs Ronninger raised would be heard time and again over the following years. The local press, in the shape of the *Hastings and St Leonards Observer* was both dismissive and condescending. Describing Madame Ronninger as the 'fair lecturer', the paper commented that she was only applauded three times, once 'for resuming her seat' and went on to say that 'the fair pleader was of prepossessing appearance, and certainly the very antitype to the strong minded women the masculine mind flinches from, at women's rights meetings generally.' The paper commented that only a dozen people had signed the petition.

Such an approach was fairly typical: women, particularly middle-class women were not expected to speak in public on political matters. Instead they were supposed to stick to their 'proper' sphere of home and marriage and leave men to deal with politics. And it was not only men who felt like this; there were plenty of women who were opposed to women taking part in politics, not least Queen Victoria who in 1870 famously wrote that it was necessary to check 'this mad, wicked folly of Women's Rights.'

The following week, an editorial in the *Hastings and St Leonards Observer* returned to the talk, stating 'the fair pleader made eloquent appeals to the "womanliness" of the ladies... but the echo, if echo there was at all aroused in the meeting was a very faint one indeed.' The editorial suggested that perhaps 'Hastings is not yet ripe for the ladies' franchise.' Hoping that the number of Madame Ronninger's converts would be as limited in other places 'as it has proved to be in Hastings', the piece finished with the view that: 'Englishmen at large hold the opinion that a woman who dabbles in politics loses much of her feminine softness and natural charms... it will take a very long time to convince the men of this country that women are in their proper sphere when "emerging from the calm path of domestic duty, they take to the stump and platform".'

> *'I hate to hear women talk politics, and I almost forget the proverbial gallantry of an Englishman to "the sex," when the said sex is represented by a petticoated spouter on women's rights.'*
>
> **Hastings Observer**
> **January 1872**

Gathering momentum

The *Hastings Observer* was correct in its view that it would take a long time to convince men that women should play a role in the political arena but quite wrong in its belief that there was little local interest, or that Hastings was not ripe for the women's vote. In fact, quite the reverse was true; there was plenty of local interest and battle lines were being drawn. Local women – and men too – started organising meetings and looked to form the first local suffrage group.

A year after Mrs Ronninger hit town, another public meeting took place. Mrs Kingsley, who was related to Charles Kingsley of *Water Babies* fame, spoke to an audience about women's suffrage. Mrs Kingsley was a local woman, who had moved to Hastings for health reasons. Her audience included a Mrs Fawcett, from

Hollington who was not related to Mrs Millicent Fawcett, but would go on to take an active role locally, and women's rights advocate and writer Anna Kingsford, a rather unusual woman for the time, who qualified as a doctor, and went on to became a committed anti-vivisectionist and theosophist. Anna Kingsford (nee Bonus) was born in Essex but went to school in Brighton. Her family also spent a great deal of time in lodgings in St Leonards where Anna's daughter Edith was born, in 1868.

By 1873 a women's suffrage committee had been formed locally. Little is known about its activities but it included a number of very interesting personalities, some of whom were already well versed in political campaigning. Caroline Fawcett and EJ Hawkes were joint secretaries. Other committee members included Mrs Bonus, the Rev JA Briggs, William Fawcett and Mrs Fawcett, Captain Fawcett, William Ransom, a radical printer who founded the *Hastings and St Leonards News* and friend of Barbara Bodichon, whose early radical articles he published, Mrs and Miss Samworth, also friends of Barbara Bodichon, Dr Archibald Shaw and the Rev and Mrs Halley Stewart. Mrs Shaw was treasurer; John Stewart was chairman. As its membership shows, this early suffrage committee was open to both women and men, something that Barbara Bodichon did not agree with, believing such societies should be women only.

Ransom and the Shaws were also involved in another campaign, namely the campaign to repeal the Contagious Diseases Acts, a series of pernicious and oppressive parliamentary acts that allowed for any woman suspected of being a 'common prostitute' to be pulled off the street and forcibly examined. If the woman was found to be suffering from syphilis, she could be incarcerated for up to nine months. Led by a charismatic and influential woman, Josephine Butler, the campaign included both women and men who fought strenuously against the Acts, risking social ostracism and physical violence for even daring to talk about sex and gender relations. Campaigners argued forcefully that the Acts punished women but not the men who were the perpetrators, a very bold stand and one that challenged the prevailing morality. The campaign not only highlighted the Victorian sexual double standard but also brought sexual behaviour into the public arena, which alienated some suffragists, who chose to distance themselves from something to contentious. Even so the campaign was featured in the local press and was ultimately successful, the Acts being repealed in 1886.

In 1871 the Manchester MP Jacob Bright had introduced a Women's Disabilities Removal Bill to the House of Commons. It proposed that women should be given the vote on the same terms as men, that is it should remove the electoral 'disabilities' that women experienced. It passed its second reading but was then defeated. He re-introduced the Bill in 1872 with the same result. In April 1873 Hastings MP Thomas Brassey was asked whether he supported Bright's bill to extend voting rights to those women who had the right to vote in municipal elections. According to the local press, Mr Brassey, while acknowledging that many women deserved the vote, said he thought that such women were in a minority and that until some considerable change 'had taken place in the general political education of the ladies he feared he should not be able to support the measure.'

His remarks did not go unnoticed and a week later Anna Kingsford wrote to the press in protest. In her letter she commented: 'I conceive that the ladies of Hastings and St Leonards will hardly feel obliged to Mr Brassey for the low estimate he is pleased to take of their intellectual standing... jesting apart...the qualification for admission to the franchise is not educational at all; it is simply the fulfilment of the duties of citizenship... the payment of the country's taxes.' It was another point that would resurface frequently in the coming years.

A few months later on 4 October 1873, what may have been the first major local debate on women's suffrage took place in St Leonards. The Rev Andrew Reed chaired the meeting. Mrs Amelia Arnold, whose husband Arthur Arnold was a prominent Liberal MP, travelled from London and gave a lecture advocating the removal of the 'electoral disabilities of women'. Also present were Miss Dunk, Messrs J Stewart, and Mrs Millicent Fawcett, who had by now established herself as a leading suffragist. Married to Henry Fawcett, MP for Brighton and a strong supporter of women's rights, Millicent Fawcett, was born Millicent Garret in 1847 and was the younger sister of Elizabeth Garrett, who went on to become the first woman to qualify as a doctor in Britain. John Stuart Mill and Barbara Bodichon had a profound influence on Millicent Fawcett who committed herself to the cause of women's suffrage and in 1866, aged only 19, became secretary of the London Society for Women's Suffrage. She would ultimately head the largest women's suffrage society in the country.

Mrs Arnold talked forcibly about the injustice that a woman who was head of the household could not vote. The meeting ended with the adoption of a petition for the 'removal of the Electoral Disabilities of Female Ratepayers'.

Just a couple of weeks later a newly formed debating society, the Hastings and St Leonards Athenaeum, held its inaugural meeting at the Castle Hotel. A men-only event, the subject for debate was 'Should the Parliamentary franchise be extended to women on the same basis as that on which is it now accorded to men?' William Fawcett presented a long and 'excellent' paper criticising the view that a woman's sphere was only in the home and arguing for the view that women as ratepayers should have the vote. He also quoted statistics to prove that the demand for this was growing. A vote was taken at the end of the talk with the majority of those attending voting in favour. The debating society frequently returned to the subject of votes for women and their debates were extensively covered in the local press, keeping the topic in the public arena.

Events such as these showed that the subject of a property-qualified woman's right to vote was being discussed in meeting halls around Hastings and St Leonards. Hardly a week passed without the *Hastings and St Leonards Observer* printing some information about votes for women, often extracting information from the *Women's Suffrage Journal*, which was launched by 1870 with Lydia Becker as editor. The *Journal* was invaluable: distributed around the country it kept suffrage societies up-to-date with the latest news and developments.

Women's suffrage meetings were taking place across Sussex. In February 1875 the tireless Lydia Becker, travelling from Manchester, spoke to a meeting at the County Hall in Lewes telling them that her society, the National Society for Women's Suffrage, had passed a resolution 'That it is unjust that those who pay taxes should be excluded from voting for Parliamentary representatives' and that women who pay taxes should have the same voting rights as they had in parish matters.

In March 1879 Leonard Courtney, MP for Liskeard and Bodmin, proposed a motion to the House of Commons that would enable women to have the vote. Sir Ughtred Kay-Shuttleworth, Liberal MP for Hastings, who was well known for his opposition voted against and the motion was rejected by a majority of 217 to 103. Until 1885 Hastings and St Leonards returned two MPs to Parliament and therefore both Thomas Brassey and Kay-Shuttleworth were MPs at this time. In 1885 the Redistribution of Seats Act came into being and from then on Hastings returned only one MP to Parliament.

Public meetings

In 1881, after much debate in the House of Keys, the Isle of Man's equivalent to the House of Commons, and pressure from the

Manchester National Society for Women's Suffrage, the Isle of Man granted the vote to property-owning unmarried women and widows. It was a landmark event, greeted with enthusiasm by suffragists and reported in the *Hastings Observer*, which quite rightly stated that the Isle of Man was the first part of the United Kingdom to recognize women's parliamentary electoral rights.

Editorials in the local newspaper stated that if a poll were taken in Hastings and St Leonards, the majority of inhabitants would be opposed to giving women the parliamentary vote. They illustrated their anti-suffrage view with what they no doubt thought was a rather witty statement that if women were admitted to government, legislation might be held up while a woman MP fed her baby – a misogynist view still around today.

However, no matter what the *Observer* thought, the early 1880s saw a marked increase in women's suffrage activities locally, reflecting the growing activism around the country, as long-skirted women everywhere began to launch suffrage societies in their localities.

On 27 October 1883 a woman's suffrage meeting took place in St Leonards at the home of Miss Fricker Hall. Miss Emma Elizabeth Fricker Hall was London-born but at some point she moved to St Leonards, where by the 1870s she was headmistress of the Hastings and St Leonards Collegiate School at Bonham House, Pevensey Road, St Leonards. Her school was run on the principles of the North London Collegiate, a school for girls founded by Miss Buss, a feminist who pioneered secondary education for girls on the lines of boys' public schools

'... if women are fit to vote for Members of Parliament they are not unfit for legislators, and then there would arise a pretty condition of things if, on the night of the Budget, the Chancellor of the Exchequer was constrained to put the House to inconvenience while she gave natural nutriment to her baby in the lobby, or a measure upon which the fate of a Government depended had to be abandoned because of the lying-in of the Prime Minister.'

Hastings Observer
April 1882

and who, with Barbara Bodichon, had been a member of the Kensington Society.

Hardly surprisingly then, Miss Fricker Hall, a staunch advocate of women's rights, hosted this meeting, which turned out to be very important. Most of those who attended the meeting were women. They included Miss Caroline Ashurst Biggs, a novelist, former member of the Kensington Society and editor of the influential *Englishwoman's Review*, and Mrs Chant, both of whom spoke in favour of women's suffrage. Miss Biggs spoke at length to the meeting, saying that her main purpose was encourage a greater interest in, and wider understanding of, the question of women's suffrage. She spelled out clearly what was being asked for: women who had the same voting qualifications as men, that is who were householders and ratepayers, should

In 1883, as usual, a woman's suffrage bill was reintroduced into the House of Commons and, once again was defeated. The recently elected Liberal MP for Hastings, Mr Harry Bret Ince QC, voted against it, even though many local women had supported his election. Suffragists all over the country kept an eagle eye on events in parliament and Ince's stand brought a swift response from feminist and trade unionist Emma Patterson, who shot off a letter to the *Women's Suffrage Journal*, which was reprinted in the *Hastings Observer*:

Mr HB Ince QC voted against the resolution within a week after his election for Hastings – an election actively promoted by Lady Brassey and her daughters...If Mr Ince desires to preserve women from... the "mire and filth of a political election", why did he accept this help?... I trust that the women of Hastings, among whom there must be hundreds of householders contributing... to the prosperity of this seaside resort, will do their best to convince Mr Ince that he walked into the wrong lobby.

have the parliamentary vote. Women were already voting in municipal elections, were being elected as poor law guardians and onto school boards: why should they not have the vote? In her view, support was growing and she was hopeful that suffragists would be able to get a clause introduced into the imminent reform bill that would give women the vote.

Following the gathering at Fricker-Hall's home, plans were made for a public meeting. Notices advertising the meeting were placed in the *Hastings Observer* and the meeting took place on 30 October in the Public Hall, Robertson Street. It was chaired by Mr T Cole, supported by among others Miss Fricker Hall, Miss Caroline Biggs, Mrs Ashton Dilke, a prominent suffrage campaigner and author of *A Treatise on Equality* (1885), Miss Caroline Biggs, Miss Stackpoole, Miss Woodgate and Mr Eiolart, a solicitor, married to Elizabeth Eiloart, a feminist who wrote for the *Englishwoman's Journal*.

The meeting, which was given huge and detailed coverage in the *Hastings and St Leonards Observer*, was very well attended. It was also wide-ranging and clear in its aims. A Third Reform Bill was imminent that would extend the parliamentary vote to agricultural workers. As explained by Mr Cole, who opened the proceedings, the proposal put forward by this public meeting was to take this opportunity to extend the parliamentary vote to women householders.

One speaker after another eloquently put the case for the woman's vote. Following the chair's introduction, Mr Elliott proposed the first resolution: 'that in the opinion of this meeting the Parliamentary Franchise should be extended to women who possess the qualifications which entitle men to vote, and who in all matters of local government have the right of voting.' Mrs Stackpoole put forward the view that the vote would increase women's interest in the world around them and stressed that women should have a voice in parliamentary decisions affecting them, rather than it being the sole prerogative of men. She also challenged a frequent criticism that women were apathetic, pointing out sharply that such apathy, if it existed, was a natural consequence of being excluded from the vote.

'It was since women had spoken in public, and since women had agitated that they had got better education for women. It was since they had done that that they had got colleges, universities and high schools opened for them...it was for them to agitate to get women properly placed on a larger scale' '

Mrs Ashton Dilke

Mrs Ashton Dilke then took the floor to say that many suffragists felt the chance of obtaining the woman's vote was better than it ever had been and that although amendments had not so far been passed, opposition in the House of Commons was decreasing. She felt progress was being made. Suffragists were holding meetings all over the country and pointing out that where once they had been laughed at, they were now being listened to. She also urged her listeners to remember that what women fought for, they achieved, giving as examples access to higher education, universities and medicine.

Following another two male speakers, Miss Caroline Biggs was the final speaker in support of the resolution. She spoke vigorously, referring to prominent men who had supported women's suffrage such as Disraeli and John Stuart Mill and once more repeated the view that if women were taxed, they should vote. She concluded to great applause by dismissing the view the women's vote would be the end of society as they knew it and urged those present to support the resolution.

A local branch

In this atmosphere of optimism a meeting was held two months later, on 17 December 1883, at Mr Cole's house, 59 Cambridge Road. The purpose of the meeting was to launch a Hastings and St Leonards' branch of the National Society of Women's Suffrage. The original committee having faded away, a new committee was formed. It consisted of Mr and Mrs Eiloart, Miss Dunk and

Miss Fricker Hall, who was elected secretary. The aim of the committee was to campaign for the vote and gain new members. The committee also included men who attended meetings, spoke at public debates and gave considerable support.

The first meeting of the newly formed committee took place on Monday January 7 1884 at 32 Havelock Road. Dr Anna Kingsford, Dr and Mrs Law, Mr John Bray, Mr CB Gabb and Mr HC Richards joined the committee and letters were read out from various supporters. Members also decided to canvass the town to gather signatures for another petition to be presented to Parliament; like public speaking, canvassing was also a daunting prospect but enabled campaigners to meet and talk with members of the public. The committee met again in February at the same address, by which time the canvass had started and subscriptions were flowing in.

This was an extremely busy time for the local suffragists, particularly in the lead-up to the third Reform Bill, which planned to extend the vote to agricultural labourers. In 1880 William Gladstone and the Liberal Party had won the general election, obtaining 352 seats and just over five per cent of the vote. Gladstone was committed to parliamentary reform and his intention was to extend the vote to men in rural areas on the same basis as men in towns and cities. It was not a popular move, being opposed by the Conservatives and Queen Victoria herself but Gladstone was determined. The Bill was introduced into the House of Commons in 1884, where it met opposition.

Suffragists around the country saw this new reform bill as an opportunity to widen the franchise to include qualified women. Supporters of the women's vote sprang into action and, just as campaigning groups do today, the Hastings and St Leonards branch of the National Society for Women's Suffrage made best use of the publicity available to them. They placed notices into the local press in advance of meetings, sent in press releases afterwards and, of course, fired off letters.

Votes for married women?

The hope was to get a clause or amendment into the third Reform Bill that would give suitably qualified women the vote. Speaker after speaker at the society's meetings emphasised the injustice of extending the vote to male agricultural labourers, who by implication were not well educated, and yet withholding it from well educated women with the necessary qualifications. By and large the call was for only property qualified single or widowed women to have the vote but there were some voices calling for married women to have the vote as well. This was a valid demand given that following the introduction of the Married Women's Property Act of 1884, married women could now be property owners, which could qualify them for the vote as well as unmarried women or widows. It was however a rather contentious issue that divided suffragists and gave fuel to opponents who argued that giving a married woman the vote would damage the relationship between wives and husbands.

On 8 March 1884 the local paper included a letter from a Mr Louis Haiter of Robertsbridge, who wrote saying that 'Women pay rates and taxes as men do, they are entitled to a Municipal vote, and that being so, what reasonable objection can we have against their admittance to the Suffrage?' Like many others, he thought the idea of women as Members of Parliament was 'absurd' but he certainly believed that 'widows, spinsters or married ladies with freehold property' should have the vote. This view was, however, countered by local committee member JG Eiolart, who wrote that it would be 'inexpedient' to include married women, quoting from a Canadian Government Bill that expressly excluded married women, whose property was held by their husbands. This however was not now the case in Britain.

Drawing room meetings

Women's suffrage was now becoming something of a hot topic: the local Parliamentary Debating Society held a very lively debate on the subject at the Castle Hotel Assembly. Mimicking the House of Commons they proposed a resolution to grant qualified women the vote, roundly debated the pros and cons, and then rejected the resolution by 60 to 35. One of the speakers, a Mr Martin, stated that his reason for opposition was 'because of the intellectual, moral and physical inferiority of women', a foolish comment quickly picked up by the local suffragists.

The local Young Liberal Association also discussed the issue, coming out in favour of the woman's vote but only for single or widowed women with the necessary property qualifications. Not surprisingly the Conservative Association, meeting in Ore, debated the topic, and in January the YMCA debated Women's Rights, and the suffrage in particular. Their meeting agreed that qualified single women and widows should be given the vote but felt that 'married women should be content to leave their political opinions to their husbands', which by and large was the received view of the time.

The local women's suffrage society met regularly, often at what were known as 'drawing room' meetings. As the name suggests, such meetings took place in the drawing rooms of various committee members, reflecting the fact that in Hastings and St Leonards the suffragists tended to come from the more middle-class educated sections of the local community.

By March the local branch had handed in several petitions to the House of Commons and announced in the press that more drawing room meetings were planned. One took place on 29 March 1884 when Emma Fricker Hall once again made her home available. Nearly 100 people attended, described by the *Hastings Observer* as a 'representative and fashionable audience.' It certainly was. As well as committee members and various other local supporters, attendees included Mrs Laura Ormiston Chant, a well-known writer and lecturer on temperance, the social purity movement and women's rights; the novelist Olive Schreiner, and Mrs Georgiana Solomon, whose husband, Saul Solomon, was an influential liberal politician in South Africa's Cape Colony. Countess de Noailles, represented by Mrs Wild, supported the meeting and its aims.

Mrs Chant, who had travelled from Suffolk, spoke passionately about the cause of women's suffrage, insisting that they were asking for the vote for those women who, 'doing the philanthropic work of the world', needed a fair representation in Parliament. Once again she stressed that they were not asking the vote for wives but for single or widowed women. Mrs Chant's speech was wide-ranging. Apart from talking about the woman's vote, she also drew attention to many barriers facing women seeking work and the attitudes of trade unions to the employment of women in hazardous and poorly paid occupations such as nail making or the sweated industries. Suffragists would return to this issue eventually claiming that the only way to help these exploited women was for women to gain the vote.

One of the members, Mrs Gant, also read out comments from Miss Matilda Betham Edwards, who was unable to attend because of ill health. Suffolk born, Miss Betham Edwards was a novelist and travel writer, who was now a Hastings resident, having moved to the town in 1869, partly for her health but also because she and Barbara Bodichon were life-long friends. A keen supporter of the woman's vote, she was particularly concerned with the importance of the vote to women tenant farmers, who under the proposed bill would be excluded, which she considered completely unjust.

Another local member, Mrs Tubbs, commented on the recent meeting of the local parliamentary debating society. She wished some of those gentlemen had been present at this

Clementina Black

Another woman concerned with the plight of exploited and so-called unskilled women workers was Brighton-born feminist and trade unionist Clementina Black. From the late 1880s she was committed to championing the rights of the lowest paid women workers such as match-girls, artificial flower makers and those in sweated trades. A committed trade unionist, in 1886 she became secretary of the Women's Protective and Providence League (WPPL), the first women's trade union. In 1888 she went as a delegate to the Trades Union Congress (TUC) and called for equal pay for equal work, the first woman to do so publicly. She went on to help unionise women in London's East End, helping to create the Women's Industrial Council. She worked closely with other Sussex women, including Hilda Martindale, who spoke on women's suffrage in Hastings, and Cicely Corbett-Fisher, daughter of Marie Corbett, a Liberal suffragist who regularly attended suffrage meetings in Hastings.

meeting, particularly the gentleman who had said women were intellectually, morally and physically inferior to men. Doubtless some men never reached the average intellect of women and she would like to have asked him at what age he would remove the vote from such a man.

In 1884 William Woodall the MP for Stoke on Trent and a firm supporter of the women's suffrage, presented a bill to Parliament, asking for an amendment to the Third Reform Bill that would give qualified women the vote. Gladstone was opposed so Miss Fricker Hall, who was an excellent letter writer, wrote to the Prime Minister, in her capacity as honorary secretary of the Hastings and St Leonards National Women's Suffrage Society. She wrote that she would be:

'greatly obliged if you will kindly let me know and authorise me to publish, the grounds on which you [Gladstone] *have come to the conclusion that the Government Franchise Bill will be imperilled by our pressing our claim in the way proposed to be done by Mr Woodall's amendment... We look at the case in this way: If, notwithstanding Government support or neutrality, the amendment should be lost, the chances of the Bill clearly would not be affected, and it must, therefore, be the success of the amendment that is feared. But it is perfectly well known that many Conservatives are in favour of it, so that if it were carried it would be by votes from both sides of the House. We may assume that all the Conservatives in the House would vote against the Bill as it stands and therefore, if they helped first to carry the amendment, their numbers as voting against the Bill when amended would not be increased. We are, therefore, driven to one of two conclusions – namely, that the Government fears some Liberals who would support the Bill as it stands, would oppose it if the amendment were carried, or it fears such increase of opposition in the Lords, owing to the carrying of the amendment as would lead to their throwing out the Bill, although they might have passed as it now stands. We cannot think that either of these results is at all likely but if you, sir, being in a position to judge much more accurately of the matter than we can do, have arrived at a contrary view, or consider that in some other manner the success of the amendment might endanger the Bill, it would be much more satisfactory to the supporters of the Women's Suffrage movement to know the grounds of your opinion than to be asked, as they have hitherto been, to abstain from pressing their claim, because it might bring about a result which does not appear to them to be at all a probable one. To put the case shortly, they do not at present see that the addition to a Liberal Bill of a clause for which many Conservatives as well as Liberals would vote, could possibly tend to increase the number of its opponents.'*

Miss Fricker Hall's letter was extremely logical and went to the heart of the matter. Even though at least 79 of Gladstone's own Liberal MPs were also pressing him to include women in the reform bill and even though in 1871, he had publicly stated that he supported women's suffrage in principle, he was facing opposition and he felt strongly that if women were included in the bill, it would fall. Not surprisingly then, Gladstone's reply, sent by his secretary, said that when Woodall's amendment came in for discussion, Gladstone would state the views of the Government in respect of the amendment and that in the meantime, the Government's line had consistently been that they would accept no further amendments to the Bill.

Miss Fricker Hall's letter was published in the *Hastings Observer*, which commented that in their opinion, she had bettered Mr Gladstone. The editor even commented that Miss Fricker Hall was doing 'very considerable service to the cause she has at heart' and that she and her 'ladies' were doing a very good job educating the public; in the paper's view they would not be surprised if the local Conservative party were won over.

Be that as it may, in June both Hastings MPs, Sir Thomas Brassey, known to be a supporter of women's rights, and Mr Ince, voted with the majority in the House of Commons and against Mr Woodall's amendment, no doubt a considerable blow to local suffragists who had supported Brassey. Gladstone also, as Millicent Fawcett described, was 'vehement' in his opposition to the amendment and to any attempt to include women in the reform bill. The decision provided ammunition to local Conservatives, who took the opportunity to attack Gladstone and his 'sheepish followers' for voting 'against the ladies'.

Miss Fricker Hall once again wrote to the *Hastings Observer*, this time enclosing a letter she had received from Mr RS Stephen, a member of the Isle of Man's House of Keys. In his letter Mr Stephens emphasized that the introduction of the women's franchise in the Isle of Man was working perfectly satisfactorily and without any problems and hoping that Parliament would soon extend to the women of England 'the privilege already enjoyed by their more favoured sisters in Mona.'

In July the local branch suspended its drawing room meetings until the autumn. Miss Fricker Hall announced that petitions were being forwarded to the House of Lords, which was then debating the Bill, and reminding readers of the paper that the society was happy to receive subscriptions.

A little mischief

There was some debate in the local paper as to whether if women gained the vote, they would also stand as Members of Parliament, something that the *Observer* considered absolutely undesirable. 'Asmodeus', author of the local notes column, visualised the scenario of a mythical Chancelleress of the Exchequer temporarily removing herself from the Treasury bench in order to attend to the needs of her children – a scenario that is still current today, even if less explicit.

An unnamed 'Hastings lady' wrote to the paper expressly stating that although women wanted the vote, they had no intention of entering Parliament, something that was challenged the following week by another correspondent who stated that the previous writer had no right to speak for all women and that such a statement reflected the view that women were still held in bondage by lifelong prejudice and that Parliament would benefit from the inclusion of women.

At this point the tireless Fricker Hall entered the fray and in August wrote to the local paper, stating categorically that 'the notion that women wish to obtain the vote to get into Parliament is a most mischievous one, constantly brought forward by our opponents and calculated to do the cause damage if encouraged.' She concluded by emphatically denying that women wanted the vote to enter Parliament, a diplomatic move given public opposition to the very thought.

Even though the local society had suspended meetings, it was still actively promoting the cause. In September the local branch republished a pamphlet by Barbara Bodichon entitled *Reasons for the Enfranchisement of Women*, which the author had first written in 1866. The pamphlet was priced 3d, and was advertised in the local paper, which described Barbara Bodichon as 'a lady who is well known to and esteemed by many old Hastingers.'

The local suffrage society had had an extremely busy year. However, despite all the petitions and pressure from some of his own MPs, Gladstone had not been prepared to accept any amendment that included women. He was already facing opposition from the Tories and the Lords and he knew only too well that if there were any amendment to the bill proposing an extension of the vote to women, the bill would fall. In the event therefore, when the bill finally became law in December 1884, about seven million men were added to the electorate but not a single woman.

CHAPTER 3

Widening Participation

'The flood tide of public opinion on this matter has set in with full vigour, and nothing – not even the rocks and shoals of masculine prejudice – can stop its onward progress.'

The failure of Mr Woodall's amendment and the passing of the Third Reform Act in the autumn of 1884 was a heavy blow for the woman's suffrage movement. Many suffragists felt particularly betrayed by Gladstone and his Liberal Party, whom several had supported because they believed the Liberals were more sympathetic to votes for women. Gladstone's explicit refusal to support the amendment and the fact that quite a considerable number of sympathetic MPs voted against, in the case of Liberals because of a strong party whip, affected the suffrage movement. It led to a slump in membership and differences of opinion over the way forward, tactics and whether or not the movement should be so reliant on political parties.

However, in other ways the defeat strengthened the women's cause, not least because increasing numbers of people began to question why women should have been excluded, given that male agricultural workers had gained the vote. Even one of the most male of organisations, the Trades Union Congress (TUC), which met in Aberdeen just before the Bill became law, had passed a motion that in their opinion the vote should be given to women ratepayers.

Gaining a foothold

Other factors also helped. In the aftermath of the Reform Act, what Millicent Fawcett described as 'new political forces' came into being that promoted the women's cause. In 1883 a Corrupt

Practices Act was passed, which made it illegal to pay canvassers and other political party workers. Previously political agents and party managers employed and paid large numbers of men to do the work of canvassing as well as clerical and other tasks. The new law banned paid canvassing altogether and limited the amount parties could spend on elections. It is still the same today. The 'fertilising shower of gold', as Millicent Fawcett described it, being withdrawn, this type of work had to be done on a voluntary basis – and who was going to do it? Not surprisingly political parties turned their attention to women and actively sought to enlist their support in these essential election-winning tasks.

The first to take the step towards deliberately including women in the business of winning elections was the Conservative Party, which in 1883 set up the Primrose League. The League's aim was to promote and spread Conservative principles in Great Britain. Its headquarters were in London. Women were included from the beginning, although within a short space of time a separate branch was established specifically for women. In 1885 a Ladies' Grand Council was launched at Lady Borthwick's home in Piccadilly, London. Subsequently local branches were formed around the country, including a branch in Hastings. Women within the League proved themselves to be excellent organisers, efficient at canvassing and very good at getting people out to vote. What's more their labour was free.

Not to be outdone, the Liberal Party also sought to officially incorporate women, and in 1886 the Women's Liberal Federation was set up with Mrs Gladstone as president and an executive committee largely made up of the wives of Liberal members of parliament. Here too the aim was to promote the aims of the Liberal Party or, as Mrs Gladstone once said, 'to help our husbands.' Significantly though, many women within the Women's Liberal Federation wanted to do more than just help their husbands – they wanted to put votes for women directly onto the Liberal Party agenda. Within a fairly short time there were many women within the Federation working towards that aim.

Carrying on

In Hastings and St Leonards, Emma Fricker-Hall and her fellow suffragists continued campaigning despite the disappointment of the 1884 Reform Act. In fact, they stepped up their efforts. They were particularly busy during March 1885, so much so that on Wednesday 18 March there were two meetings, one in the afternoon and one in the evening. The first took place at Mr Nevill's home, 30 Wellington Square. Mr TH Cole chaired the meeting and those present included Miss Charlotte Biggs, Emma Fricker Hall, the Eiloarts and Mrs Fanny Cecilia Tubbs. Mrs Tubbs, who was usually described as Mrs Colonel Tubbs in the local press, probably because she was married to a Colonel Robert Tubbs, an Indian Army veteran and local philanthropist, was a much respected supporter of women's rights and later secretary of the local examination board.

Miss Biggs addressed the meeting, moving a resolution that the meeting should send a petition to Parliament to pass a measure extending the vote to women. She talked about the progress that women had made over the previous fifty years and asked why it was that women should not have the vote. She also urged women to take up the opportunities available to them such as seeking election to the local board of guardians, stressing how important it would be for the borough. Mrs Tubbs seconded the resolution and also suggested that women should form a local Women's Ratepayers' Association to look into issues affecting women. The resolution was carried and the meeting ended.

Elizabeth Blackwell

Elizabeth Blackwell was yet another distinguished woman to make Hastings her home. She was born in England in 1821 but her family moved to America when she was about eleven. Her father having died, she, her sisters and her mother opened a school in Cincinnati to support the family. She developed an interest in medicine and in particular becoming a doctor, believing that many women would prefer to be treated by a female doctor rather than by a man.

Given male hostility, she was rejected by 29 medical schools but in 1847 was finally accepted at the Geneva Medical School in New York. The male students ostracised her and teachers prevented her from attending medical demonstrations but despite these barriers, she graduated first in her class in 1849, becoming the first woman to qualify as a physician in the United States. She studied midwifery in France, where she contracted an eye infection that left her without sight in one eye.

She returned briefly to England in 1850, where she became the first qualified woman doctor on the British Medical Register; she also met and inspired Florence Nightingale and Elizabeth Garrett Anderson, who themselves became medical pioneers. Returning to America, she worked in the New York slums, opening a dispensary for women and children, and provided health care for women during the American Civil War (1861–65).

She returned to England in 1869, moving to Hastings in 1879 where she leased Rock House, Exmouth Place. She was a well-known figure, attending public meetings and giving support to the women's suffrage campaign. She died in Hastings in 1910.

Hard on the heels of this meeting, a second took place in St Leonards that evening, this time in Miss Fricker Hall's drawing room. Anyone who has been involved in organising campaign meetings will know just how exhausting this must have been for Miss Hall and the other organisers. These, however, were determined and strong-minded women, absolutely committed to their cause and if that meant exhausting themselves, so be it.

The meeting was well attended by both women and men and Dr Elizabeth Blackwell, who had been living in Hastings since 1879, moved what was a rather wordy resolution: 'That as the function of Government tends increasingly to control details of private as well as public life, thereby influencing education, industry, morality and sobriety, it becomes the duty of women, Christians and citizens, to increase those votes which they already possess, and to claim the extension of the Franchise, in order to maintain a due influence on social and political action.' Interestingly, Dr Blackwell stated that she was more firmly behind the first part of the resolution and somewhat sceptical of the second part, feeling, as she commented, that women were not making nearly as much use of their municipal vote as she thought they should.

Mrs Eiloart also spoke and was extremely critical of Gladstone's failure to support women's suffrage, indicating that many suffragists would think long and hard before offering him their support again.

Changing minds

March 1885 had been an extraordinarily active time for the local branch, something commented on in the *Hastings and St Leonards Observer*, which noted that the local branch 'does not seem inclined to let the grass grow under its feet in its pursuit of the "rights of the sex".' Startlingly, Asmodeus, the author of the local notes column in the *Hastings Observer*, also commented that he had 'at last become a convert to the doctrine I once despised,' not least because it was an anomaly to bestow the vote on 'two millions of farm hands, while twenty thousand lady tenant farmers were declared in the same breath to be unfit to exercise an identical franchise.' Asmodeus also remarked that he felt it would help the cause for the local society to move out of the drawing room and hold more meetings in public.

In late March Mr Ince MP, presented a petition to the House of Commons in favour of the woman's vote, which had been adopted at the recent drawing room meeting. In April Thomas Brassey did likewise. Ever the inveterate letter writer, Miss Fricker Hall wrote to Brassey in August urging him to support Mr Woodall's Bill, now down for its second reading and hoping he could now support it. Rather strangely, however, Brassey, despite supporting women's suffrage, wrote back saying he felt it was desirable to delay any decision until after the general election – a disappointing turn of events for local suffragists. In the event, the second reading of Woodall's bill was adjourned four times and never reached a vote. Woodall re-introduced a women's suffrage bill again in 1887, 1889 and 1891 but always without success.

Local suffragists such as Miss Fricker Hall kept in close contact with the national organisations, which, equally, were aware of what was happening on the south coast. As one of the leading lights in the local women's suffrage campaign, Miss Fricker Hall, together with Barbara Bodichon and Elizabeth Blackwell, were among the signatories to a letter that the National Society for Women's Suffrage sent to the House of Lords urging the extension of voting rights to women. The *Hastings Observer* reprinted one paragraph from the letter, which they stated was 'sweetly brief and almost masterful in its terseness and logical cogency'. In this paragraph the writers of the letter, who included Millicent Fawcett, stated that among those who would be excluded under the Third Reform Bill were:

'women landowners, who form one-seventh of the land proprietors of the country; women of means and position living on their own property; schoolmistresses and other teachers; women engaged in professional, literary, and artistic pursuits; women farmers, merchants, manufacturers and shopkeepers; besides large numbers of self-supporting women engaged in industrial occupations. The continued exclusion of so large a proportion of the property, industry and intelligence of the country from all representation in the Legislature is injurious to those excluded, and to the community at large.'

The argument could not have been clearer and even the *Hastings Observer* admitted that, having originally opposed the movement, the paper was now minded to wholeheartedly accept the principles of the women's suffrage demands – a fairly dramatic shift of attitude.

Fighting on other fronts

While activists in Hastings were primarily focused on campaigning for the woman's vote, they also involved themselves in a range of other issues relating to women's rights, such as the continuing inequalities for women in higher education. In January 1888 Dr Elizabeth Blackwell and a number of well-known local suffragists, including Miss Betham-Edwards, Barbara Bodichon and Mrs Tubbs were among many women who signed a memorial (statement of facts supporting a petition) that was sent to the Vice Chancellor and Senate of Cambridge University. Their demand was that women students graduating from Cambridge should be awarded their well-earned degrees, just as men were. The female students had attained the necessary academic achievements, so why were they not awarded a degree? The signatories stated that 'under the existing regulations, women do not become members of the university, and though they may have satisfied every condition which entitles an undergraduate to a degree, the degree itself it withheld.' The University of London had awarded degrees to women in 1878 and they argued, 'on ground of justice and expediency, that to all, without distinction of sex, who fulfil the prescribed conditions, the same recognition should be accorded...it is felt to be a discouragement to women desiring to pursue their studies at Cambridge, that the academical status granted by other universities is denied to them.' Male fellows of other universities sent a letter in support but to no effect. It was not until 1920 that Oxford University formally awarded degrees to women – and Cambridge University finally did so in 1947.

Going public

The *Hastings Observer* had suggested that local suffragists might like to consider speaking to a wider public rather than confining themselves to drawing room meetings, and this they did. In January 1888 a meeting in support of the woman's vote was held in the Public Hall in Hastings. Mrs Millicent Fawcett was billed as the main speaker. The event had been widely publicised in the local press, as was another public meeting due to take place at much the same time, a visit from the Liberal Unionist MP George Goschen.

Taking the opportunity to make a point, Elizabeth Eiloart wrote to the press drawing attention to the fact that Mrs Fawcett's meeting was open to both women and men, and was free of charge, while only men were invited to Goschen's meeting and had to pay 3 shillings. Even if they paid, only a very limited number of women would be accommodated in the gallery. Mrs Eiloart commented that she was aware that some of the Liberal Unionists supported women's suffrage but they had to put their party first and they knew their support would only come from men, 'why the women, poor things, must go to the wall, as they have often had to before…no slight is meant, no injury inflicted upon us only a little disappointment, and the feeling that though many of our number are householders and ratepayers, we are placed somehow on a lower level than the sterner sex – non-voters, non-existent for political purposes…' She finished her letter by hoping that Mrs Fawcett would have a cordial reception and reminding her readers that men, women, voters and non-voters were all welcome, that there would be no special gallery for anyone and admission was free.

The meeting itself took place on Thursday 26 March. Mrs Millicent Fawcett, or Mrs Henry Fawcett was she was usually described – it was normal for a married woman to be referred to by her husband's name at that time – was given a very warm welcome. Mrs Tubbs, Miss Fricker Hall and Elizabeth Blackwell supported her on the platform and in the hall as did other members of the Hastings and St Leonards Suffrage Society. The hall was absolutely packed, with women making up the bulk of the audience. No exact figures are available but according to the *Hastings Observer*, every corner of the room was full, indicating just how important the subject was and how keen local people were to hear Mrs Fawcett speak.

Mrs Fawcett spoke at length about how the situation had changed over the last twenty years and how supporters of the women's suffrage should congratulate themselves for the progress that had been made. When John Stuart Mill had first raised the matter in 1867, only 70 members of Parliament had been supportive. Now, she estimated 343 members from all parties supported votes for women. Also the various political parties were calling on women to get involved and support their party. She felt that there was now a general feeling that it was only a matter of time before women gained the vote and that public opinion was moving in their direction.

Their cause had supporters in both the political parties and she had no doubt that the 'glacial drift of English opinion' had moved and was moving in the direction of the active participation of women in politics. Mrs Fawcett argued that women's involvement in politics could only be a force for good. It was only necessary to look, for instance, at the work that women were doing as school inspectors and on boards of guardians to see the important role that women could play and she challenged the view that men could represent women on the grounds that they were actually different. She pointed out that much of women's political campaigning was to do with what many might see as domestic issues such as temperance, social purity, housing for the poor, education and so on. For this was indicative of how important women's role in politics was and she said she had little doubt that real improvements to the lives of women and children would only come about once women had the vote. She sat down to rapturous applause, her long speech having been frequently interrupted by cheers from the audience.

'If men and women were exactly alike, the representation of men would represent the women – but not being exactly alike, that wherein they differed was unrepresented in the present system.'

Millicent Fawcett, 1888

The same themes were picked up and expanded on by the speakers who followed and the meeting ended with a resolution that 'in the opinion of this meeting, the Parliamentary Franchise should be extended to women who possess the qualifications which entitle men to vote, and who, in all matters of local government, have the right of voting.' The resolution was carried and the meeting ended.

A few days later an editorial in the *Hastings Observer* expanded on the point that Mrs Fawcett had made, namely that attitudes had changed. Referring to a speaker twenty years earlier, coincidently also called Mrs Fawcett but a resident of Hollington, the paper commented that when that Mrs Fawcett had raised the issue of the woman's vote, it 'aroused but the faintest interest among the local community...and her printed contributions were... read with a feeling of amused wonderment... so few ladies, save the small minority, cast in a specially courageous mould, were to be found urging... equal political rights with men.' Today, however, when Mrs Henry Fawcett, 'the eminent advocate' of women's rights spoke on the platform, she not only addressed an audience that supported her but also, via the press, had the satisfaction of speaking to thousands of sympathisers outside the hall.

In 1889 various local suffragists were among 2,000 women who added their names to a declaration in support of women's suffrage that was issued by the National Society for Women's Suffrage. Local signatories included veteran campaigners Miss Fricker Hall, Mrs Tubbs, Elizabeth Blackwell, Miss Beetham Edwards, Barbara Bodichon and Mrs Eiloart. However there are very few references to either drawing room or public meetings of the local women's suffrage society in 1888–89. Miss Fricker Hall left the area and it is possible that, as sometimes happens, the departure of a woman who had clearly been a powerful driving force, weakened the group, which probably disbanded around this time. However, what had been happening locally was also happening nationally. For the moment the fight seemed to have gone out of the suffrage campaign. Over the previous thirty years or so hardly a year had gone by without meetings, debates and petitions or resolutions in support of women's suffrage; the issue was firmly on the political map but the Reform Acts of 1867 and 1884 had failed to include votes for women, while private members bills put forward by 'friends in the House', such as Mr Woodall had also failed to get women the vote. Membership of suffrage societies dropped and between 1885 and 1904 the House of Commons only voted twice on the issue of the woman's vote.

Political involvement

Women's political activism however was far from declining. In fact, from the late 1880s an increasing number of local women became involved in political work of one sort or another. In May 1886 a local branch of the Primrose League was formed. The inaugural meeting took place at the Royal Concert Hall, Warrior Square. One of the main speakers was Mrs Lucas Shadwell, who was subsequently appointed president of the local branch. Mrs Lucas Shadwell was an author and resident of Fairlight. In a stirring inaugural speech, she outlined the role of women in the League: 'We women can do much... It is rather the custom of our opponents to laugh at us, but I flatter myself we have some influence, and we mean to use it... We can canvass, distribute leaflets, and assist in registration, by seeing that all those who have a right to vote are put on the register.' Mrs Lucas Shadwell and her colleagues carried out these tasks highly efficiently and in 1895 her husband, William, was returned as MP for Hastings.

The Primrose League met regularly in Hastings and St Leonards over the next ten or more years and attracted a sizeable membership from local Conservative women. It also hosted social events: the *Hastings Pictorial Advertiser* frequently printed photographs of members of the Primrose League in long skirts, hats, and high collared blouses hosting garden parties and events for families and children. Mrs Lucas Shadwell was a popular and highly respected speaker and president who supported votes for propertied women, declaring in 1888 that 'our great leader, Lord Salisbury, has declared himself in favour of Female Suffrage, so we may hope before long it will be granted to women of property...fifteen to twenty per cent of the houses in this country are occupied by unmarried women and widows... representation should accompany taxation...why should not woman have a voice in the questions which touch her country's welfare.' The issue of votes for women was frequently discussed at meetings although it was made absolutely clear that members of the Primrose League were expected to unequivocally support and work for Conservative candidates whether or not the men supported votes for women.

A Hastings and St Leonards branch of the Women's Liberal Association (WLA) was launched in 1892, which attracted a large number of women supporters of the Liberal Party. The local Women's Liberal Association was extremely active during the 1890s and well into the early years of the 20th century, often liaising with Liberal women from elsewhere in Sussex, including Bexhill and Brighton. Local activists in the Association included Mrs Slade, the president of the Hastings branch, Mrs William Ransom and Mrs Jane Strickland, a firm believer in votes for women who went on to become a highly respected campaigner for the cause in the period leading up to the First World War. Described by the *Hastings Observer* in her 1932 obituary as 'one of the greatest educational and social workers that Hastings has ever known', Mrs Strickland also served on the Hastings School Board, and in 1901, became one of the first members of the Hastings Education Committee, education being a lifelong passion. She was also a member of the Workers Educational Association (WEA) and was involved with various charities and initiatives for vulnerable and disabled children. For many years, Mrs Strickland was a committed Liberal, believing the Liberal Party to be the greatest and only reforming party but increasingly saw votes for women as her greatest priority, which saw her joining the National Union of Women's Suffrage Society (NUWSS). She became increasingly disillusioned by the Liberal Party, believing they had betrayed women, and, after the First World War when she was in her 70s, joined the Labour Party. Her husband was a corn and seed merchant; the family business, which started in 1818, finally closed its Silverhill shop in 2017.

The WLA held women-only meetings around the different districts of Hastings, including Ore, Halton and Clive Vale, which were usually well attended. Meetings included not only local and visiting speakers but also musical interludes. Meeting halls were consistently beautifully decorated with flowers and flags in the colours of the Liberal Party and songs, recitations, tea and cake invariably accompanied political debate.

'The government of the world by men alone has not been such a distinct success as to recommend the continuance of an exclusive system which has its basis in the 'subjection of women'

Annual Report of the Borough of Hastings Women's Liberal Association August 1892

The issue of votes for women was a constant theme of the Association's meetings and by 1894 it was becoming clear that many members wanted the Liberal Party to commit to giving votes for women. In September 1894 delegates from the Women's Liberal Associations of Sussex met in Hastings in the Wellington Square Baptist schoolroom. Lunch and tea were provided. Delegates came from all over the county. They included, from Brighton, Louisa Martindale, a very active member, committed to improving the lot of working-class women and a powerful advocate of the women's suffrage. Marie Corbett was the East Grinstead delegate. An active suffragist, whose husband was a Liberal MP, Marie Corbett campaigned for the women's vote in East Grinstead and Uckfield. Neither area was sympathetic to votes for women and on one occasion Marie Corbett found herself pelted with rotten fruit for daring to stand up in the High Street with her daughters demanding votes for women. Hastings' delegates included Mrs Strickland, Mrs Slade, Mrs Lile, Mrs Shaw, and Miss Duffield. Mrs Payne from Cuckfield gave an earnest speech in favour of making votes for women a party priority and, in contrast to the Primrose Society, a resolution was passed urging women to do everything they could to secure Liberal parliamentary candidates who supported the woman's vote.

Opposition

Despite the *Observer's* editorial, there was still plenty of opposition to women's involvement in politics. In May 1895 the paper printed a letter from a Mr WHB of 15 Wellington Place, who was clearly appalled by the possibility of women in government. He grudgingly acknowledged that it was probably inevitable that women would gain the vote but pointed out that women being in the majority, there was a danger that the Government of this county would change from a masculine one to a feminine one and urged his readers to 'Think what this will mean; bear in mind how totally different are the masculine and feminine methods of procedure...He must be a bold man indeed to say that in the main women are now equal to men, either in breadth of mind, originality of thought, freedom from prejudice, ability to weigh and consider evidence...' He concluded by stating that he, for one, looked 'with fear and distrust on such a violent change as handing over the controlling power of the State to women.'

Around this time also anti-suffragists were becoming far more visible, vocal and organised. In 1889 Mrs Humphrey Ward, an author in the highly sentimental Victorian style, published *An Appeal against Female Suffrage*, an article in which she appealed to the 'common sense and the educated thought of the men and women of England against the proposed extension of the Parliamentary Suffrage to women.' In her view 'the struggle of debate and legislation', the running of the country, international affairs and the organisation of the armed forces belonged to men. For both physical and cultural reasons, women had no place in these areas; for Mrs Ward, chasing after equality with men would diminish 'women's true dignity and special mission.' Mrs Ward's article was very influential and within just a few years the Women's National Anti-Suffrage League was formed.

A long way off

By the 1890s women all over the country were gaining influence and independence. Working-class women were entering trade unions while middle-class women were working as inspectors, on school boards and as poor law guardians. They could vote in local councils and had also overwhelmingly proved themselves to be politically competent. Women's involvement in the Primrose League and the Women's Liberal Association gave the lie to the old idea that politics was not a suitable activity for women. There could no longer be any question of keeping women out of politics – they were already there.

However, despite nearly 40 years of patient campaigning, letter writing and petitioning, to say nothing of packed meetings both in drawing rooms and public halls, women had still not gained the vote. Divisions had appeared within the women's suffrage movement, particularly over the issue of which women should have the vote. By and large most private members bills excluded married women, which distressed some suffragists who believed this could make marriage an explicit bar to political rights and suggested that married women's civil rights were inferior to those of their single or widowed sisters. In fact in 1892, Gladstone used just this argument when explaining his opposition to one of Woodall's bills, writing 'The Bill is a narrow Bill, inasmuch as it excludes from its operation the entire body of married women; who are not less reflective, intelligent, and virtuous than their unmarried sisters.'

Mrs Fawcett, Lydia Becker and most of the Hastings suffragists believed that only unmarried women, whether single or widowed, should be eligible for the vote; they believed giving married women the vote might cause domestic disharmony – they also probably believed it was politically expedient to stick to this narrow stand. Other suffragists though believed all qualified women – married or single – should have the vote. As a result various suffrage campaigners, among them Mrs Josephine Butler and Emmeline and Richard Pankhurst, formed the Women's Franchise League in 1889 to include all suitably qualified women. And finally there were those who wanted 'universal suffrage', the vote for all women and men over 21, a call that would become louder with the emergence of Labour Representation Committee (LRC) in 1900. Six years later the LRC became the Labour Party.

There were also disagreements about the relationship of the women's suffrage movement to political parties, which would continue for several years, and which intensified as suffragists gained a greater hold within the Liberal Party, through the Women's Liberal Federation. In 1888 the women's suffrage movement split into the Central National Society for Women's Suffrage, which supported the affiliation of women's Liberal societies, and the Central Committee of the National Society for Women's Suffrage, which stayed politically neutral.

For now it felt as if a stalemate had been reached: the tried and tested methods of peaceful campaigning had won support within the House of Commons and among large sections of the public but the government was not shifting. In 1893, overcoming resistance from many male MPs, women in New Zealand gained the vote. One year later women in South Australia won their vote after intensive campaigning and similarly in 1899 women in Western Australia gained the vote. But in Britain successive Conservative and Liberal governments remained intransigent. Mr WHB of 15 Wellington Place, Hastings, should not have been so alarmed: the women's vote was still a long way off. And as for handing over the control of the State to women; as recently as the 2017 general election there were still only 208 female MPs out of a total of 650. Clearly the British women's suffrage movement had to look for new campaigning directions and methods.

CHAPTER 4

Deeds not Words

'Every sort of constitutional and "womanly" method has been pursued... but, so far, this has failed.'
Jane Strickland

As the Victorian era drew to a close – Queen Victoria died in 1901 – and the new century approached, the women's suffrage movement seemed to have reached an impasse. However, a number of events occurred that galvanised the movement and took it in new and often far more forceful and dramatic directions. The fact that women in New Zealand and South Australia had gained the vote gave new hope, while growing support from working-class women, particularly in the north of England, also helped to energise the suffrage campaign. In addition the 1895 general election had returned a large number of MPs – over half – pledged to the principle of women's suffrage. Naturally not many suffragists put much faith in election pledges but they gave some hope.

The years leading up to the First World War were thrilling and often turbulent as thousands of women all round the country flocked to the cause, making 'Votes for Women' one of the leading and most pressing political issues of the day. Actresses, shop assistants, clerks, mill workers, university students, aristocrats, trade unionists, socialists, Liberals, Conservatives, middle-class and working-class women alike threw themselves into what became an increasingly bitter struggle. From the early years of the new century, long-skirted women everywhere, often faced with hostility and contempt, held public meetings, sold suffrage newspapers on the street, chalked pavements and heckled politicians. Increasingly visible in public, they marched, demonstrated and even went to prison in their absolute determination to get the vote.

New organisations were launched whose strategies and campaigning methods often differed radically. There were two main strands. The first and by far the largest were the suffragists, who organised in the National Union of Women's Suffrage Societies (NUWSS), which was launched in 1897 with Millicent Fawcett as its elected president, a post that she held until 1919. The NUWSS merged together the National Central Society for Women's Suffrage and the Central Committee for Women's Suffrage, in effect acting as an 'umbrella' organisation that brought together virtually all the existing women's suffrage societies, as well as attracting thousands of new recruits. Local suffragist Marie Corbett, from Uckfield, was on the Executive Committee. The NUWSS was run on democratic lines; its members, known as suffragists, believed in using peaceful, law-abiding methods to achieve their aim – the parliamentary vote for women. It was based in London, produced its own newspaper, *The Common Cause*, and by 1914 had a membership of some about 100,000 women in branches all over the country.

The second strand were the suffragettes, militant women who organized in the Women's Social and Political Union (WSPU). Founded in Manchester, the WSPU was set up in 1903 by Emmeline Pankhurst and two of her daughters, Sylvia, a socialist and artist, and Christabel, a law student. Mrs Pankhurst had campaigned for the women's vote for many years, having set up the Women's Franchise League with her husband, the radical lawyer Dr Richard Pankhurst. He died in 1898 and after a while Emmeline returned to campaigning. She had been closely linked to the Independent Labour Party (ILP) but left disillusioned because they prioritised adult rather than women's suffrage. She also broke with the NUWSS believing their traditional and peaceful campaigning methods would never achieve votes for women. What was needed was a new society and to this end the WSPU was launched with the aim of 'immediate enfranchisement' by 'political action', a commitment to 'Deeds not Words' and a determination to gain the vote 'by any means necessary'. Unlike the NUWSS, the WSPU was to be women-only but like the NUWSS would campaign for the parliamentary vote for women 'on the same terms as it is, or shall be granted to men'. The WSPU also produced its own newspaper, *Votes for Women* and later *The Suffragette*.

From its beginnings the WSPU, which at its height probably had around 5,000 members, was run on fairly autocratic lines like a voluntary army, with instructions coming down from the top, although as time went on some of the more dramatic actions were initiated by individual members acting independently. In 1905 the WSPU hit the headlines when Christabel Pankhurst and Annie Kenney, a young mill worker from Oldham, were thrown out of a Liberal Party election meeting for standing up, unfurling a banner

'I invited a number of women to my house in Nelson Street, Manchester, for purposes of organisation. We voted to call our new society the Women's Social and Political Union, partly to … define its object as political rather than propagandist. We resolved to limit our membership exclusively to women, to keep ourselves absolutely free from party affiliation, and to be satisfied with nothing but action on our question. "Deeds, not Words" was to be our permanent motto'

Emmeline Pankhurst

on which was painted the soon to be famous slogan 'Votes for Women' and asking 'Will the Liberal Party give votes to women?' Bundled out of the meeting, they were arrested and imprisoned, giving the cause more press coverage than it had received in 40 years. The WSPU moved headquarters to London and continued to adopt an increasingly militant approach to campaigning, interrupting political meetings, heckling politicians, storming the House of Commons and devising ever more imaginative actions. Its members, who adopted the name 'suffragettes' after the word was used as an insult in the *Daily Mail*, began to be arrested and imprisoned, which together with their dramatic strategies, kept votes for women constantly in the news.

The militancy of the WSPU annoyed and even alienated many in the wider suffrage campaign, to say nothing of the general public, who were in the main absolutely horrified by their tactics. As time went on other organisations also emerged, including the Women's Freedom League, which formed in 1907 as a breakaway group from the WSPU. Artists, writers, actors, sympathetic men and others also formed their own suffrage societies.

Liberal women continue campaigning

Against this background, women in Hastings and St Leonards responded to developments and redoubled their efforts in the fight to gain the vote. Stalwart suffragists such as Jane Strickland, Mrs Slade, Matilda Betham-Edwards and Mrs Tubbs, who consistently supported peaceful campaigning, continued to raise the issue of women's suffrage at public and other meetings, often through the Hastings branch of the Women's Liberal Association (WLA). The WLA met regularly and their meetings were always reported in the *Hastings Observer*.

In 1902, Mrs Slade, now president of the local WLA, gave a stirring speech to a packed meeting in the Public Hall, Robertson Street, saying that no matter what tune the Liberal Party played 'the keynote must be Women's Suffrage'. Another key figure during this period was Mrs Marie Freeman-Thomas, daughter of Sir Thomas Brassey, Liberal MP for Hastings from 1868-86. In 1892 Marie married Mr Freeman-Thomas, who in 1900 was elected Liberal MP for Hastings. They lived in Old Hastings House. Steeped in Liberalism and a staunch supporter of votes for women, as was her husband, Marie Freeman-Thomas attended and spoke at many meetings in support of the women's suffrage. So too did Mrs Felton Smith, who in 1902 stood up at a meeting of the Sussex Union of Women's Liberal Associations to argue that the Liberal Party should adopt votes for women as an integral part of the Party's political programme.

Women such as Jane Strickland stepped up their demands. Disappointed by the fact that the Liberal Party was not committing absolutely to votes for women, a new organisation, the Women's Liberal Federation (WLF) was formed and by 1903 its members, who included Mrs Strickland, were making it their special business to press for the suffrage at every opportunity. Mrs Strickland went on to join a group within the WLF, known as the Forward Suffrage Union, which by 1909 was calling for Liberal women to refuse to work for Liberal candidates who were not prepared to prioritise votes for women – a far cry from the original aims of the Women's Liberal Association.

'When the politicians give us women the right to work in the fields of the nation's affairs, we will work. While they deny it, let us all, Conservative, Liberal, or what not, take them at their word and go on strike.'

Mrs Jane Strickland, 1909

A new suffrage group

On 16 April 1904 a packed meeting took place in the Princess Room of the Royal Concert Hall, Warrior Gardens, St Leonards. The meeting, which was under the auspices of Millicent Fawcett's NUWSS, brought together both Liberals and Tories, attracting women from the Women's Liberal Association and the Primrose League, as well as a number of men.

Several well-known campaigners were present, including Mrs Freeman-Thomas, Mrs Strickland, Matilda Betham-Edwards and Mr and Mrs William Ransom. Also present were Mrs Darent Harrison and Mrs and Miss MacMunn, who were to become significant names in the local suffrage movement. Born in 1855, Isabella Darent Harrison was an accomplished novelist

65

and musician. She and her husband, an artist, had arrived in the area about three years earlier and lived at 1 St Paul's Place, St Leonards. She had been an advocate for votes for women for many years – her mother and Millicent Fawcett were good friends – and was, according to the local press, 'pleased to have settled in our town, which she regards as quite a stronghold of the Women's Suffrage movement'. Not surprisingly, she had thrown herself eagerly into the local campaign.

Mr Freeman-Thomas, who opened the meeting, said how pleased he was to address such a 'cosmopolitan' gathering, in which all political parties were represented. He re-emphasised his support for women's suffrage and reminded everyone that the aim of this meeting was to set up a local branch of the Central Society for Women's Suffrage. Other speakers followed, including Mrs Betham-Edwards who said she thought she might be the only person there old enough not only to have heard 'the illustrious pioneer of women's suffrage' John Stuart Mill but also to have spoken to him. The meeting passed a resolution, 'that…it is injurious to the best interests of the country, and contrary to the just principles of representation that women be excluded from the Parliamentary Franchise. It [the meeting] therefore pledges itself to do all in its power to forward the just claims of women to full citizenship.'

Following this meeting a new suffrage society was formed. Cecilia Tubbs was chosen as president, while Mrs Freeman-Thomas was vice-president. The society, which stressed it was non-party political, later became a local branch of the NUWSS. It held regular meetings and its members supported law-abiding methods to achieve the vote.

A political spat

The local newspaper was now regularly publishing letters about votes for women as increasing numbers of local people

– and not only local – put pen to paper to voice their views. The overall impression in Hastings and St Leonards was that it was mainly Liberal women such as Mrs Strickland who were pushing the issue. In May 1905 a woman wrote in who signed herself 'a Conservative women's suffragist'. She stated it was not only Liberal women who were fighting for the vote but also Conservative women, who likewise were putting pressure on their party. Against the background of the Boer or South African War, which had ended in 1902, she asked whether it was not time 'for the party that drew the sword for freedom and free institutions in the Transvaal to consider the claims of the women who helped supply the sinews of war...'. For the benefit of 'those of your readers who have never taken Women's Suffrage seriously, and are under the impression that it is only advocated by a few eccentric females', she went on to list a number of privileged women who supported the woman's vote.

The *Observer*, being something of a right-leaning periodical, picked up on this letter to make an attack on the Liberal Party claiming that the way in which the Liberal Party was attempting to champion the cause of women was 'amusing to the thoughtful student of politics' and that it was advocating for women only to score political points. In the paper's view many local Conservative women and Primrose Leaguers were just 'as anxious about the rights of women, as the lady Radicals'.

This sort of political point scoring was not surprising given a general election was coming up. Up and down the country, suffragists and suffragettes were challenging parliamentary candidates to give their views on votes for women, with suffragettes focusing particularly on the Liberals. Suffragists in Hastings and St Leonards followed suit and wrote to the local candidates to get their views. Jane Strickland wrote to Mr Freeman-Thomas, who was the sitting Liberal MP, asking whether he was in favour of granting the vote to women. A known supporter, he replied that, 'any woman who pays rates and taxes should be entitled to a Parliamentary vote' and that he would support any measure in the House of Commons to that end.

Mrs Darent Harrison wrote to Harvey du Cros, the Conservative prospective parliamentary candidate. His answer was ambiguous. He said that he had already been asked the question when his candidature was announced at an all male meeting and he had commented that he had no doubt that the men present supported the idea. He also wrote that he sympathised with Mrs Harrison's views but said nothing about doing anything practical.

The 1906 general election resulted in what is usually described as a 'Liberal landslide'. The Liberals with Sir Henry Campbell-Bannerman at their head swept to power, throwing out Arthur Balfour's Tory government. Hastings however decided to buck the national trend, electing the Conservative, Harvey du Cros and throwing out Mr Freeman-Thomas. Interestingly, the 1906 general election was the second in which the Labour Representation Committee (LRC) fielded candidates; they won 29 seats and shortly afterwards the LRC changed its name to the Labour Party.

Going public

With the arrival of a Liberal Government, a wave of optimism swept through the NUWSS and its supporters. With so many men now enfranchised, there was little possibility of another electoral reform bill so what women wanted was a specific woman's suffrage bill. Local suffragists such as Mrs Strickland, Mrs Slade and Mrs Betham-Edwards had always believed Liberalism would or should include the woman's vote and now the Liberal Party was in power, they assumed it would enfranchise women. Their assumption did not however take into account that although many Liberal MPs supported the woman's vote, the party was divided over the issue, not least because they feared that if women gained the vote, they would vote Tory.

In May 1906, Jane Strickland travelled from Hastings from London to join a deputation of some 500 women to see the newly elected Prime Minister, Henry Campbell-Bannerman and urge him to introduce a woman's suffrage bill. The deputation included women of all classes from millworkers to students. Most were members of the NUWSS but also present were Emmeline Pankhurst and Mrs Emmeline Pethick-Lawrence, key figures in the WSPU. Mr Campbell-Bannerman told the group bluntly that while he personally might support votes for women, his cabinet would not, and that his government was unlikely to introduce legislation for female suffrage.

To say this was a disappointment would be an understatement: suffragists locally and nationally had worked for the Liberal Party, which had now effectively betrayed them. The WSPU, who had never put much faith in the Liberals anyway, adopted increasingly dramatic tactics to draw attention to the cause. From now on there could be no reliance on 'friends in the House'; the focus of actions was the government and individual MPs. In October suffragettes protested at the House of Commons and there were several arrests, a pattern that would be repeated many times. The protest increased publicity for the cause but there were many who disapproved; the *Hastings Observer* for instance was full of critical comments.

Stalwart campaigner Jane Strickland always remained a suffragist but she admired the Pankhursts and believed they were 'the moving spirits' in a new campaign. She was not afraid to state her views publicly and put pen to paper in a very articulate letter, writing to the *Hastings Observer* in October 1906 'to say a word on behalf of the so-called suffragettes who are at the present moment calling attention – as some think by very unwise methods – to the great question of the Enfranchisement of Women. Though not a member of the Women's Social and Political Union...I nevertheless feel that the women who are conducting the campaign are stirred... by a great and pressing sense of the disabilities which thousands of their poorer sisters especially suffer... by lack of the Parliamentary vote... they are fighting pluckily and strenuously for what they believe to be one of the most needed political reforms of the day... all who agree with them on the main question should hesitate before condemning... their action... Is it not fairer to look upon them... as the Advance Guard of the movement... and if unable to agree with all the methods they are pursuing at least to recognise that their cause is ours...they are at least willing to suffer for their convictions...'

> 'The movement began 40 years ago; every sort of constitutional and "womanly" method has been pursued to gain this right for the women of England, but, so far, this has failed...Is it to be wondered at that some earnest souls have become utterly impatient... If their zeal has carried them a little too far, let us at least be patient with them.'
>
> **Jane Strickland**

While the WSPU was becoming increasingly militant, heckling politicians, disrupting political meetings and going to prison, the NUWSS, though continuing with their petitions and local meetings, also looked for bolder and more obvious means of attracting support and publicity. Campaigning moved into the public arena, with an increasing number of open-air demonstrations taking place in London. The first major suffrage demonstration took place on 7 February 1907 and was called by the NUWSS. More than 3,000 women, led by Millicent Fawcett, marched through cold muddy streets from Hyde Park to Exeter Hall to call for the vote. Hastings activist Jane Strickland took part in the march, which was later nicknamed the 'Mud March' because of the appalling weather and the mud that caked the women's long skirts.

Suffragettes come to Hastings

In Hastings and St Leonards campaigning was also stepping up. A Hastings letter writer calling herself 'Liberty and Equality' described the suffragettes as 'brave, noble women' and applauded their 'bold stand' at the House of Commons. She urged all women in Hastings to heckle their MP Harvey du Cros and 'inspired by the sufferings of our sisters who have suffered the horrors and degradation of prison...band together... to show man we are his superior and that we shall have votes for women.' As it happens, du Cros was not in favour of votes for women.

By 1907 suffragettes were arriving on the Sussex coast where they disrupted a meeting on Free Trade held in the Brighton Dome. Lord Brassey, whose wife Lady Sybil de Vere Capell was later president of the local NUWSS spoke without interruption but when Reginald McKenna MP the Minister for Education began to speak, suffragettes who had placed themselves among the crowd began to heckle him. Stewards rushed forward and forcibly ejected the women one after another. As one woman was thrown out, so another stood up and heckled before being forcibly removed. Twenty suffragettes were treated in this way; men who tried to prevent the violence were also physically attacked.

On 23 February 1908 Hastings was plunged into a Parliamentary by-election following the announcement that Harvey du Cros was resigning his seat because of ill health. His son Arthur du Cros was speedily adopted as the Conservative candidate.

A day or two later, in advance of the by-election, there was a near riot in Hastings when three WSPU leaders – Christabel Pankhurst, Flora Drummond and Nellie Martel – arrived to hold an open-air meeting in Wellington Square. The meeting took place at 7.30pm and had been advertised via the town crier; there were no advance notices in the local press. When the women arrived by cab in the rain, they found a large crowd of boys and young men waiting for them together with uniformed and plain-clothes police. There was also a large crowd around the square. When the women began to speak, the mob greeted them with 'ironical cheers, derisive laughter and cat calls'. Nothing daunted, Flora Drummond and Nellie Martel continued trying to make themselves heard. Pieces of orange peel began to fly towards them and the police insisted the women leave the square immediately. They refused to do so. Christabel Pankhurst then got up onto the makeshift rostrum and started speaking. At this point someone began to hurl eggs at her and the crowd surged forward. As the mood grew nastier, the police dragged the three women out of the square, fighting a pathway through the crowd and escorted them downhill to the Castle Hotel.

A reporter from the *Hastings Observer* interviewed the three suffragettes shortly afterwards. He found the women unhurt but disgusted by the behaviour of the crowd. They were equally displeased with the authorities for not providing them with proper facilities, such as a lorry to stand on. Christabel Pankhurst was annoyed with the police for dragging them away because it gave the wrong impression and if they had been given more time she believed the crowd would have listened. On the reporter commenting that they might have been hurt, Christabel Pankhurst replied, 'Well, we risk that every day.'

Three other suffragettes arrived in Hastings the following day to provide reinforcements and more meetings took place over the next two days in local schools. A few local councillors attended and there was some heckling, but no violence.

Correspondence flooded into the local paper following events in Wellington Square. One writer, signing herself 'A Surprised Visitor' expressed surprise at the lack of local suffragist support for the visiting suffragettes: 'I was present on Tuesday evening, when two of these ladies bravely tried to address an open-air meeting in Wellington Square and were so disgracefully treated by a set of Hastings hooligans...I was astonished that they had not with them a large body of the local Suffrage Society...who ought to have rallied round the speakers. If they had a dozen or two around them to keep back the roughs, other respectable persons in the crowd might have had a chance of getting nearer...' It was a fair comment but equally it is possible that because the meeting had not been advertised in advance, local suffragists may not have known about it.

Events continued apace. Local suffragists opened an office at 31 White Rock with the specific aim of making suffrage literature available to the public. Subsequently a local Women's Suffrage Society was formed, which was independent of political parties.

On March 26 suffragettes came to Hastings again. This time the meeting was advertised in advance through the local press, which announced that the speakers would be the 'celebrated' Mrs Martel and Miss Christabel Pankhurst. The meeting took place in the afternoon at the Royal Concert Hall and was for women only. Two male reporters and Mr Slade were the only men present. The hall was packed with local activists, including Jane Strickland. There would probably have been others who came out of interest. It was announced that Christabel Pankhurst and Nellie Martel were unable to attend because of ill health; however Mrs Emmeline Pankhurst, founder and leader of the WSPU had come instead.

WSPU activist Miss Lambert opened the meeting, explaining what the suffragettes wanted and why they had adopted militancy. She said it was not a pleasant experience to be thrown out of a Cabinet Minister's meeting but the time had passed for women to behave properly. Mrs Pankhurst then took the floor. A very charismatic woman and excellent speaker, she outlined the work and impact of the WSPU and spoke eloquently on the need for equality between the sexes and the vital importance of women gaining the vote. She

Suffragettes on the beach, 1908

talked about their actions at the House of Commons, even describing the events leading up to her most recent arrest, causing laughter and applause when she asked: 'Do I look like a woman who would be so foolish as to fight with a big policeman?' She concluded by urging the women of Hastings and St Leonards to take their part in the fight.

A second meeting took place that evening, also at the Royal Concert Hall, to which men were admitted. Miss Lambert chaired and calmly referred to the way in which the press misrepresented the suffragettes, commenting on occasions when she had peacefully left a meeting only to read the next day that she had been carried out kicking and screaming. Mrs Pankhurst addressed much of her speech directly to the men in the audience, arguing that men had mismanaged politics so making women's involvement essential. A number of young men at the back of the hall heckled and interrupted, causing Mrs Pankhurst to comment how sad it was to see such young men so badly brought up and badly educated, which caused another outburst of yelling. Eventually the youths quietened down and Mrs Pankhurst took questions.

In April suffragettes interrupted a packed Liberal Party meeting in the Royal Concert Hall, St Leonards. The first suffragette heckled the speaker, Mr Sydney Buxton, demanding votes for women. She was forcibly ejected from the meeting. Five other suffragettes did similarly and one by one each was dragged out of an increasingly chaotic meeting. Once the women had been forced out of the hall, Sydney Buxton stated that, as a cabinet minister, he had voted for women's suffrage but given the events of the evening, he did not consider that WSPU members were worthy of the vote. His comments were published in the *Hastings Observer*. The following week, Christabel Pankhurst wrote to the *Observer* saying, 'We should be more impressed by this remark did we not know that for the past forty years statesmen have traded on the quietness of women and have ignored their patience and constitutional agitation. It is only now… when women have asserted themselves that any attention whatsoever is paid by Cabinet Ministers to the Women's Suffrage movement.'

> *'You see when we behave ourselves they take no notice of us, and we are not going on like that any more'*
>
> **Miss Lambert, WSPU**

Scolds and viragos

These events made the news and the local newspaper was flooded with letters for and against votes for women. Many criticised the suffragettes, accusing them of unacceptable and unfeminine behaviour. One anonymous letter writer, signing himself Barrister-in-Law, lammed into the suffragettes, describing them as 'common scolds and viragos, who are fortunate to live in an age which has forgotten the use of the ducking stool.' However the writer's main concern was that if women gained the vote on the same basis as men, it would enfranchise prostitutes because 'the vast majority of these unfortunates would have the lodger's vote.' According to Barrister-in-Law's research there were at least 200,000 prostitutes in Britain, 50,000 or 60,000 of them in London so that – horror of horrors – there might even be London constituencies where 'these unfortunates' held the elections in their hands.

Cartoons from the *Hastings Pictorial Advertiser* lampoon the suffragette

Jane Strickland was quick to respond through the *Observer's* letter page, commenting that she 'thought that every conceivable argument for and against women's suffrage had already been advanced... but your correspondent [Barrister-in-Law] unearths yet one more! He would apparently impose a morality test in connection with the extension of the franchise to women.' Quite rightly she suggested that if this were the case, perhaps 'Barrister-in-Law should advocate the withdrawal of the vote from all men whose private life is on a level with that of the women that he holds up to such scorn.'

Hard on her heels came a woman from London, signing herself A Barrister's Wife, who wrote into the *Hastings Observer* stating that 'to apply to women voters... a law of sex morality that has not applied to men voters is manifestly unfair and ridiculous...' The *Observer* received so many letters in response to Barrister-in-Law that after two weeks, it announced it would take no further responses.

Suffragettes had caught the public attention in a way that suffragists had not. Their impact was not always positive but it was certainly powerful. Increasingly, local schools produced plays that featured or included stereotypical suffragettes. The 'rage of the afternoon' at the Clive Vale Council School's annual prize giving programme was a portrayal of a suffragette meeting that featured twenty schoolgirls waving banners.

> 'When a local natural history lecturer asked a school child: 'Where is the Amazon?' she promptly replied, 'In Holloway.'
>
> **Hastings and St Leonards Observer**
> **27 April 1907**

Popular and music hall entertainment, particularly on Hastings Pier, also featured portrayals of suffragettes. These were usually humorous and mocking and were very well received by locals and visitors to the town. According to the *Hastings Observer*, the hit of one evening on the Palace Pier, St Leonards, was 'Johnny' Hunter's suffragette sketch, which caused a 'lively and hilarious time'.

On the crest of a wave

On 13 June 1908 several suffragists from Hastings and St Leonards, including Mrs Harlow Phibbs, secretary of the Hastings and St Leonards branch of the Central Society for Women's Suffrage, Isabella Darent Harrison, Lettice MacMunn, Beatrice Wilson, Mrs William Slade and Mrs Strickland, travelled together by train to London to take part in a huge demonstration organised by the NUWSS. At least 10,000 women, and probably many more, assembled on the Embankment. Then, led by Millicent Fawcett they marched along Northumberland Avenue, Lower Regent Street and Piccadilly to the Albert Hall. Information about the demonstration, or procession as it was called, first appeared in *The Times* on 8 May and within days the Hastings and St Leonards suffrage group had decided unanimously that the branch needed to be represented at such an important occasion. As one of them commented, they wanted to show that Hastings and St Leonards was not lagging behind in the fight.

Timed to coincide with the International Conference for Women's Suffrage just about to begin in Amsterdam, the procession was made up of women who were determined and confident in their demand for the vote. They came from all over the country: they included professional women, university women, teachers, artists, musicians, writers, business women, nurses, members of all political parties, trade unionist, members of the Women's Co-operative Guild, married women, single women, barmaids, shop girls, and factory workers. Women were organised into eight different sections or 'blocks'. The Hastings and St Leonards branch marched in the first block, which included all the provincial NUWSS societies or branches. The Artists' Suffrage League, particularly Mary Lowndes president of the League, designed stunningly beautiful silk banners that were carried by women at the head of each section.

The procession, which was two miles long, was a mass of colour and banners. Marie Corbett and Mrs Conybeare, who both visited Hastings regularly, wore scarlet and white sashes and helped to marshal the first section, followed by Mrs Strickland who was one of the stewards. She later said, 'what impressed me most was the attitude of the crowd. Seven bands marched with us...but the most inspiring thing was the remarkably sympathetic attitude of the onlookers'. She compared it to the Mud March, 'when the crowd seemed to look upon the whole thing as a joke, and there was a great deal of jeering. This time the crowd showed better manners...men took off their hats... one was heard to say "Fine lot of sportswomen; I wish 'em luck." At the end of the procession, Millicent Fawcett, dressed in academic robes, took the chair for the rally in the Albert Hall, which was absolutely packed. 'Now, I trust, we are on the crest of the wave,' said Mrs Strickland hopefully.

Nine days later, on Sunday 21 June, a smaller contingent of local women travelled by specially organised excursion train from Hastings, Warrior Square or West Marina to Victoria Station in London – price 2s return – to join a mammoth demonstration which had been called by the WSPU. Herbert Asquith, who was by now prime minister, had said his government might consider a women's suffrage bill provided it could be proved that enough women wanted the vote – the WSPU's intention was to provide the proof.

The demonstration was advertised well in advance. The *Hastings and St Leonards Observer* publicised the event and provided details of trains and routes. The day before the event, two young suffragettes, wearing 'votes for women' sashes also held open-air meetings at the Fishmarket in the Old Town and in Warrior Square. As yet, a local WSPU had not been set up in Hastings and St Leonards but some local women were members. Among them were Elsie Bowerman and her mother Edith Bowerman Chibnall, both of whom lived at Thorncliff, London Road, St Leonards. They were very active in the WSPU and in May 1908 Mrs Edith Chibnall presented the WSPU with a beautiful silk banner for the demonstration, which had been produced locally. Writing to thank Edith Chibnall, Mr Pethick Lawrence said: 'we shall treasure your banner for many years to come. It will lead us to victory.' Another local WSPU member was Miss Forbes Robertson of 44 Chapel Park Road, St Leonards, who had been converted to the cause by Mrs Pankhurst when she had spoken in Hastings.

On 21 June, the Hastings and St Leonards contingent arrived at Victoria to be greeted by bands, banners and stewards who directed the group to their place in the march. The demonstration, which became known as Women's Sunday, was extremely well organised. Over thirty special trains had been laid on to bring campaigners to London from all over the country. Seven separate processions of around 30,000 women, each headed by its own banner, including the one from Hastings, converged on Hyde Park from different parts of London. Several bands accompanied each procession and within each procession different groups carried their own banners, in all a total of 700 banners. Everywhere the WSPU colours of purple for honour, white for purity and green for life predominated. Some West End stores, such as Dickens and Jones in Regent Street, reported that they had sold out of dresses, gloves and hats in the WSPU colours, which does indicate the fact that most of those present were middle-class or from privileged backgrounds. In Hyde Park itself there were twenty separate platforms for speakers, who included Emmeline Pankhurst, Keir Hardie, Mrs HG Wells, Mary Gawthorpe and other notables. Speakers began to address the vast crowd at 3.30 in the afternoon and at 5pm a bugle 'heralded in the great shout: Votes for Women.'

The demonstration was massive. Estimates suggest that there were between 300,000 and 500,000 people in Hyde Park; it was the largest women's suffrage demonstration to date. It had, however, absolutely no effect on Prime Minister Asquith, who remained completely intransigent and steadfastly opposed to giving women the vote. Hardly surprisingly therefore suffragettes stepped up their militancy, rushing the Houses of Parliament, and finding ever more dramatic ways of challenging the government. Arrests and brutal treatment of suffragettes also intensified.

Muriel Matters and Violet Tillard in the Women's Freedom League van

© *Mary Evans Picture Library*

Muriel Matters arrives

1908 was quite a year. In July Emma Townsend, a St Leonards resident, announced that a local branch of the Women's Anti-Suffrage Association had been formed. Taking its inspiration from Mrs Humphrey Ward, the local branch invited those women of Hastings and St Leonards 'who are opposed to the mischievous Votes for Women movement' to join the Association and mount a counter campaign.

At the opposite end of the suffrage spectrum however July saw the arrival in Hastings of the Women's Suffrage Van and Muriel Matters, an Australian-born activist who would eventually make Hastings her home. Born in Adelaide in 1877, Muriel Matters was a successful actress and elocution teacher. In 1905 she left Australia for London, where she taught elocution, gave recitals and occasionally earned money as a journalist. She interviewed anarchist Peter Kropotkin, a meeting that she said changed her life. Kropotkin challenged her to put her skills to better use and, already interested in 'the woman question', she became involved with the British women's suffrage movement. At first she attended WSPU lectures and meetings but in 1908 joined the Women's Freedom League (WLF). The WLF was an interesting organisation. In 1907 there were disagreements in the hierarchy of the WSPU, particularly over the increasing autocracy and elitism of Emmeline and Christabel Pankhurst. As a result, Charlotte Despard and some 70 other WSPU members left to form the Women's Freedom League. Like the WSPU its members were militant, in that they were prepared to break the law, but it was run on democratic lines and was opposed to attacks on property.

Muriel Matters soon became a well-known figure in the WLF. Together with others, she took part in high-profile protests against Winston Churchill, another politician determinedly opposed to giving women the vote, which gained her some publicity and established her as a bold activist and skilled speaker.

In May 1908 the WLF decided to send Muriel Matters with a veteran campaigner, Lilian Hicks, to the south-east in a horse-drawn wagon, travelling from town to town to spread the word, attract new members and set up new branches. The two women and their wooden van, which was painted green and emblazoned with the words Women's Freedom League and Votes for Women, set off from Charlotte Despard's home in Surrey on 16 May. They arrived in Hastings on 14 July, by which time another suffragist, Violet Tillard, had joined them. The women held an open-air meeting at Wellington Square on the evening of the 15th and a second open-air meeting at the Fishmarket the following evening. The weather was dreadful and the women retreated into the actual market, only to be pelted with fish heads and entrails. Nothing daunted, the women continued to address the crowd about the importance of the vote and the injustice of paying tax without having representation, which was a strong WLF line. The next day they moved on along the coast to Eastbourne. Following the van's visit to Hastings, Mrs Darent Harrison became a member of the WLF.

On 28 October 1908 Muriel Matters made news headlines when, in an audacious protest she effectively became the first woman to speak in the House of Commons. Together with her colleague Helen Fox, she had taken a seat in the Ladies' Gallery in the House of Commons, which was available for women who wanted to watch parliamentary proceedings provided they behaved themselves. She chained herself to the metal grille, as a symbol of male oppression, and gave a speech in which she said that women had sat behind 'this insulting Grille for too long... it is time that the women of England were given a voice...we demand the vote.' Helen Fox, similarly chained, then spoke, while Violet Tillard unfurled a banner, which proclaimed that the Women's Freedom League demands votes for women. There was complete chaos: police and attendants arrived and grabbed Muriel but finding that the chains were locked, were forced to remove her still attached to the grille, which they unscrewed. Eventually the chains were sawn through.

As it happened, a Hastings resident, Norman Jepson of Robertson Street, was in the Strangers' Gallery when the protest took place and gave his account of events to the *Hastings and St Leonards Observer*, who published it. Describing the events, he said that he 'heard the shout which suddenly startled the House and then I saw the ladies standing up in the Grille...I could not see that they were chained from where I was, but when the attendants came I could see there was something wrong, because they did not remove the women at once...There seemed to be a lot of confusion and struggling...and all the time one of the women was speaking...Then there came a crackling sound, and I saw a portion of the Grille being pulled away bodily. Shortly afterwards the ladies disappeared in the midst of a struggling group...'

Little did Mr Jepson know that the woman was Muriel Matters and that she would in years to come be a well-known Hastings resident. She moved to Pelham Crescent in Hastings during the 1920s and stood unsuccessfully as a Labour candidate for Hastings in 1924.

The local suffrage group

As the year drew to a close the Hastings and St Leonards branch of the Women's Suffrage Society held a public meeting on 21 November in the small ballroom of the Royal Concert Hall, St Leonards. Pretty well all the experienced local suffragists were present: Mrs Harlow Phibbs, Mrs Darent Harrison, Miss Lettice McMunn and Mrs Strickland, as well as Miss Jebb, Miss Ruth Kenyon, Miss Russell and other women. There were apologies from the society's president, Mrs Tubbs and also the guest speaker, artist Mary Lowndes, who had a bad cold.

Ray Strachey, who had travelled from London, gave a stirring speech, saying that if someone from Mars dropped suddenly into their midst, the first question would be: 'Why do women not have votes?' In her view there were no grounds whatsoever for refusing to give women the vote. She spoke eloquently also about women in the sweated industries, describing how their lives were becoming increasingly difficult. Many of these women did not own a home, so that unless qualified women gained the vote, these women would have no one to speak for them.

During the course of the meeting Mrs Harlow Phibbs explained that members of the group had decided to form an independent organisation – the Hastings and St Leonards Women's Suffrage Society. Mrs Darent Harrison immediately offered to make her home available for meetings three afternoons a month. Clearly local activists were still fully committed to fighting for the vote. The next three or four years would see ever more dramatic actions taking place in Hastings and St Leonards.

CHAPTER 5

Frustration grows

*'We are women fighting as women for
the enfranchisement of women.'*
Mrs Darent Harrison

From 1909 the campaign for the woman's vote became increasingly bitter. As government intransigence frustrated women's efforts to gain the vote, suffragists continued with so-called constitutional or law-abiding methods, which included refusing to pay taxes. Members of the WSPU upped their militancy, smashing windows and, as time went on, firebombing property. Police brutality also intensified: as women rushed the House of Commons or made other protests, they were beaten and dragged off to prison. By 1910 more than 600 women had served prison sentences; by 1914 the figure had reached a thousand. Imprisoned women demanded their right to be treated as political prisoners, a demand that the Home Office consistently refused. In protest, in 1909, Marion Wallace-Dunlop became the first suffragette to go on hunger strike; many other suffragettes followed her example. In the same year, future Hastings resident Muriel Matters took to the sky in a hot air balloon to scatter Votes for Women leaflets over London, an imaginative and dramatic stunt that captured the public imagination.

New societies

In Hastings and St Leonards campaigning intensified with public meetings, 'at homes' and a growing number of out door events. New suffrage societies emerged. The earlier suffrage society became a local branch of the National Union of Women's Suffrage Societies (NUWSS) and in March 1909 the Hastings, St Leonards and East Sussex Women's Suffrage Society was formed. Miss Stanham of Wysall Lodge, St Leonards was secretary, and veteran campaigner Mrs Tubbs president. In 1913 Miss Kate Rance of 21 Boscobel Road took over the post of secretary. Mrs Jane Strickland was chair, or chairman as she would have been described then. Always active, she was also president of the Bexhill branch of National Union of Women's Suffrage Societies (NUWSS) and later chair of the Free Church League for Women's Suffrage.

'It is said that the attention of the Medical Officer of Health is being called to a new virulent disease that has recently taken root in Hastings, and is being shamelessly spread far and wide throughout the town by a band of energetic and enthusiastic ladies. "Suffragitis" is the name given to the new disease, and the ladies who are responsible for its propagation in Hastings are glorying in the fact that a very large number of people have shown themselves peculiarly susceptible to its attack.'

Hastings and St Leonards Observer, 11 December 1909

Some tensions developed within the local suffrage campaign, partly because some suffragists felt the Women's Suffrage Society was too closely linked to the Liberal Party, particularly through Mrs Strickland. As a result, a second society was launched later in the year – the Hastings and St Leonards Women's Suffrage Propaganda League. Mrs Darent Harrison was the secretary and the moving spirit behind the new society, which was independent of all political parties and not affiliated to any of the big central societies, whether militant or non-militant. Quoting Isabel Willis, one of the League's active members and a frequent letter-writer to the local press, the League was formed 'for the purpose of peaceful propaganda in our borough.' Its aim was to educate the public about women's suffrage and what women wanted. Committee members included Mrs Charlotte MacMunn, who was the treasurer, and her two daughters, Lettice and Nora. Members were suffragists and believed in law-abiding tactics. Mrs Darent Harrison, described by one of the League's members as, 'a lady of a very fighting disposition', strongly supported direct action in the form of tax resistance. She became a member of the Women's Tax Resistance League (WTRL) when it was formed in 1909. Encouraged by Mrs Darent Harrison, the local League adopted the policy also.

By December 1909 both societies had acquired local offices. The Hastings, St Leonards and East Sussex Women's Suffrage Society opened an office at 29 Havelock Road, Hastings. Miss Shrimpton ran the office, which displayed suffrage posters, sold suffrage literature and was used for meetings and lectures. Miss Shrimpton stressed that the Society was law abiding, saying, 'we may not agree with the law as it is made by men, but we intend to abide by it till we have the power ourselves to alter it.' The Hastings and St Leonards Women's Suffrage Propaganda League opened their office at 47 London Road, St Leonards. Again, the office space was used for meetings and offered literature and information about the women's suffrage movement. Both offices were a hive of activity. Women also sold copies of *The Common Cause* on the seafront, while copies of the WSPU's journal *Votes for Women* were available, price 1d, from King Bros newsagent, next door to the main post office.

Mass meetings

Each society held weekly meetings, sometimes at their offices or in their homes. Mrs Darent Harrison regularly organised campaigning 'at homes' at her house 1 St Paul's Place, St Leonards, while Mrs Strickland similarly made her home Halstead available. Public meetings were organised at various venues around town. The Royal Concert Hall in Warrior Square, which had been built in 1879, was a popular venue not only for concerts and other entertainments but also for suffrage meetings. Each society invited guest speakers, some of whom were well known activists. In March 1909 the Royal Concert Hall was crowded to overflowing to hear Dr Flora Murray speak. A medical pioneer and member of the WSPU, she helped to treat suffragettes injured at demonstrations or coming out prison. During the First World War she and her close companion Elizabeth Garrett Anderson would set up military hospitals in France. Mrs Strickland also spoke at this meeting, commenting that women of all classes were now joining the campaign. She said that a friend was serving time in Holloway and whether or not they approved of militancy, 'they must respect women whose courage made them feel that prison had no terrors.'

Another huge meeting took place in April 1909, this time at the Public Hall in Robertson Street. The speakers were Mrs Ethel Snowden, a leading suffrage campaigner, whose husband Sir Philip Snowden was a socialist and Labour MP, and Mr Baillie-Weaver, a well-known barrister and member of the Men's League for Women's Suffrage. A local branch of the Men's League was set up around this time. Mrs Harlow Phibbs of the Women's Suffrage Society together with others organised a women's suffrage choir, which sang suffragist songs before the meeting began.

> 'The women's suffrage movement is the biggest and strongest movement in the political and public life of today.'
> **Mrs Snowden**

October 1909 saw another large suffrage meeting at the Public Hall. The meeting, which was hosted by the Hastings, St Leonards and East Sussex Women's Suffrage Society, started at 4.30pm so that teachers could attend. All the usual campaigners were present: Mrs Tubbs, Mrs Strickland, Miss Mosley, Mr and Mrs Slade, Miss Norton, who had come from Bexhill, Mrs Darent Harrison and Miss Ruth Kenyon. The guest speaker was Mrs Alys Russell, whose husband, philosopher Bertrand Russell, had stood unsuccessfully as a Women's Suffrage candidate in Wimbledon in 1907. The meeting was so crowded that everyone had to be moved to the larger upper hall, causing Mrs Strickland to ask: 'who can say that Women's Suffrage is dead in Hastings?'

Local press reporters seem to have attended every meeting, whether it was an 'at home', a suffrage garden party, or a huge public meeting, and their reports are impressively detailed. Articles in the press always list the names of those who attended and the same names re-occur: Mrs Strickland and Mrs Darent Harrison feature prominently not just in reports but also in the letter pages of the *Hastings Observer*, so much so that on one occasion in 1912 the paper's letter page was headed with the words 'Another letter from Mrs Darent Harrison.' Other names crop up frequently: Miss I Willis, Mrs MacMunn and her daughters, Mrs Harlow Phibbs, Miss Mosley, Miss Reckitt, Mrs Burnier, Mrs William Slade, Miss Russell, Miss Bullock, Mrs Ruth Kenyon and a host of others whose names are not well known today but would have been so at the time. There were regular male supporters also, including Lieut-Colonel Savile, of the Men's League for Women's Suffrage, Councillor T Reed, Mr Strickland, Councillor Felton Smith and William Slade. It is difficult to know the exact membership of the societies, although Miss Shrimpton is on record as saying that the Women's Suffrage Society had at least 100 members. Supporters frequently came to Hastings from Bexhill, Rye and Winchelsea, which also set up their own suffrage societies.

Conciliation Bill

1910 was election year. Mrs Strickland declared her intention to 'set the whole town ablaze' – metaphorically speaking – and to concentrate on making sure that local candidates, if returned to parliament, would commit to votes for women. Suffrage campaigners paraded through St Leonards in a carriage decorated with a large yellow banner demanding votes for women, while other women stationed themselves at polling stations. This was a new tactic – when men turned up to vote, women invited them to sign a petition in favour of votes for women. Some men refused but according to the local press the majority of electors were happy to do so. The petition was very successful: some 1600 signatures were collected and the petition was sent up to Westminster to be added to others from around the country. According to Millicent Fawcett, more than 280,000 signatures were collected countrywide on polling day.

The Liberal vote was well down and the election resulted in a hung parliament, with Asquith and the Liberals having to rely on the support of Labour MPs to form a government. In Hastings Arthur du Cros, known for his anti-suffrage views, held his seat comfortably with an increased vote. Votes for women was now a major political issue in Britain and one that no government could ignore. A majority of MPs in the new parliament actually favoured votes for women, although there were big disagreements on how this was best achieved and which women should be enfranchised.

In February 1910 an inter-party Conciliation Committee for Women's Suffrage was set up consisting of 25 Liberal MPs, 17 Conservatives, six Irish Nationalists and six Labour MPs. The chairman was Lord Lytton, whose sister Constance was an active member of the WSPU, served four terms of imprisonment and underwent the torture of forced feeding. Henry Brailsford, left-wing journalist and one of the founder members of the Men's League for Women's Suffrage was the Committee's secretary. The Committee put together a bill, known as the Conciliation Bill, which was to extend the franchise to 'women occupiers'. It was a compromise, designed not to alienate any political party and would only have enfranchised about one million women.

Despite reservations, suffragettes and suffragists supported the Bill as the best on offer at that time and the WSPU called a truce to militancy. High profile campaigning continued in order to keep the issue in front of the public and to ensure that MPs everywhere knew that women were demanding their rights. Weekly meetings took place in Hastings and St Leonards and women such as Miss Willis, Mrs Strickland and Mrs Darent Harrison wrote constantly to the local press with arguments in favour of female suffrage. The letters make fascinating reading: they are passionate, informed, well argued and beautifully written. Nor did they lack in humour, particularly when it came to criticising anti-suffragists, who also wrote to the local press, stating that women were not suited to politics and deploring the actions of militant suffragettes, described by one speaker as 'turbulent spinsters'. Interestingly anti-suffrage writers rarely gave their names; instead they preferred to remain anonymous, using made up names such as 'Annabel' or 'An Anti-Suffragist'. Annabel was a particularly frequent and often vitriolic letter writer.

In July 1910 Edith MacMunn and Isabella Harrison jointly sent a letter to the local press in which they referred to the fact that Asquith had urged MPs to vote against the second reading of the Conciliation Bill on the grounds that there was no great demand for the vote amongst women. They commented that the Bill had passed its first reading with a majority of 109 and asked, 'how comes it that 299 Members of Parliament supported the Bill, while only 190 could be induced to oppose it, if women are as indifferent or the electorate is as hostile as the Prime Minister would have us believe? The answer is obvious. The Prime Minister is wrong. It is the opponents and not the Women's Enfranchisement who represent the indifferent minority in the country.' The writers appealed to 'those who have as yet taken no active part in the movement to come forward.'

On 18 June 1910 Mrs Strickland, Miss Stanham, Miss Sadler and other local women joined a huge suffragette march and rally in London's Trafalgar Square. As usual the procession was a mass of banners, bands and women wearing the WSPU colours of green, white and purple, often in the form of a tri-colour sash draped across a white dress. A feature of the march was a contingent of more than 600 women, all dressed in white, wearing prisoner's medals and carrying 'a glittering host of steely broad arrows,' representing their time in prison.

The Conciliation Bill passed its second reading in July 1910 and the NUWSS organised a huge rally in Hyde Park on the 23rd July. Once again local women took part, mainly from the Hastings and St Leonards Propaganda League. Mrs Isabella Darent Harrison, Edith Chibnall, Mrs de Guerin, Lettice MacMunn, Miss Crabbe and Miss Parr were among the local women who marched behind the banner of the local League. Commenting on the event, Isabella Harrison said, 'those who were privileged to take part…know that to all intents and purposes the women householders have already won their citizen rights.'

Unfortunately this statement was over optimistic. The Conciliation Bill passed its second reading with an increased majority but was then shelved as Asquith called a second election. He promised that provided the Liberals were returned the Conciliation Bill would once more be debated in the new session of parliament. On 18 November 300 women led by Emmeline Pankhurst marched to the House of Commons to protest. For more than six hours women were met with the most horrific violence and sexual assaults from the police and attacks from bystanders. In the end 115 women and four men were arrested. The attack was so shocking that suffragettes remembered the event as 'Black Friday.' It has been said that this one event possibly illustrated more than ever the consequences for women when they tried to enter what was considered to be an exclusively male space.

In Hastings too the government's attempt to kill the Bill had sparked a fresh outburst of activity. A series of open-air meetings were held on the beach near the Fishmarket. The first to speak on the beach was Anna Munroe of the Women's Freedom League (WFL) who held her audience for over an hour. People were reluctant to leave so she took questions and a collection box was passed around.

On 25 September local WSPU activists together with members of the Women's Propaganda League organised a women's suffrage parade. The aim was to publicise an upcoming meeting at which Mrs Pethick-Lawrence and Mrs Mary Jane Clarke, Emmeline Pankhurst's younger sister, were to speak. Lettice MacMunn and one or two other women from the

Top: Elsie Bowerman leads local suffragettes in procession.
Below: Mrs Darent Harrison and Mary Clarke follow in carriage.
Hastings Pictorial Advertiser, Sept 1910

League were first to arrive at the Memorial, where they waited for suffrage friends from Bexhill and Mrs Darent Harrison, who arrived in an open carriage bearing the words: 'Women's Suffrage Propaganda League.' Sitting with her was Mrs Clarke. About twelve women marched in single file, while the carriage brought up the rear. WSPU activist and barrister Elsie Bowerman led the march carrying a green flag together with her mother, Edith Chibnall, a great admirer of Mrs Pankhurst. Women from Winchelsea and Bexhill joined the procession, carrying banners saying 'No Surrender' and 'Face to the Dawn'. The procession moved off from Robertson Street and marched along the seafront past Warrior Square, up London Road, through Kings Road and Western Road, back along the front and up Queen's Road, returning to the Memorial at 1pm. There were a few jeers but in the main passers-by were respectful, some men raising their hats.

Three days later, Mrs Pethick-Lawrence and Mrs Clarke, who would die in December after being force fed in prison, addressed a large meeting at the Royal Concert Hall. Elsie Bowerman presented Mrs Pethick-Lawrence with a huge bouquet of flowers and the local women's suffrage choir sang. Mrs Pethick-Lawrence asked whether it was fair that in a town such as Hastings, where the majority of people were women who made their living by letting lodgings or catering for visitors, women might have to pay election expenses or the salary of a man who did not represent them. She caused considerable laughter by poking fun at anti-suffragists and finished by saying that the WSPU's militant methods were 'milk and water' compared with what men had done when they were trying to get the vote.

By this time a branch of the Women's Anti-Suffrage League had been formed in Hastings, and in November a heated debate broke out at a drawing room meeting in St Leonards, attended by suffragists and anti-suffrage campaigners. The room was packed and feelings flared when the anti-suffragists stated they had conducted a postcard poll that indicated nearly 80 per cent of the local population were opposed to women having the vote. The speaker referred to the 'turbulent spinsters who were making the life of Cabinet Ministers unbearable' and asked whether they should be allowed to tell their husbands how to vote – a rather odd question.

Following Black Friday, the Women's Suffrage Propaganda League held an 'indignation' meeting at 5 Grand Parade, St Leonards to protest the brutal treatment meted out to the women's deputation to the House of Commons. Lettice MacMunn had been present at the event and described the scenes in Parliament Square. As an eyewitness she said she could testify to the 'orderliness and dignity of the women until brutally attacked by the police.' Mrs Darent Harrison and

Local suffragists on election day, Dec 1910. *Hastings Pictorial Advertiser*

Mrs Chibnall had also been part of the deputation, and sent letters describing the events. The meeting passed a formal resolution protesting the treatment.

In December another general election took place. The local women's suffrage society sent questions to the parliamentary candidates for Hastings (Arthur du Cros) and Rye (Mr G Courthope). Du Cros wrote back saying that married women should definitely be excluded from the vote and that in his opinion, the issue was so important it should be put to the country in the form of a referendum, though he did not use the word 'referendum'. Courthope, replying to Mrs Strickland, stated that 'so long as violent disorder and agitation continues on the part of a section of those seeking for the franchise', he would do nothing to help the Women's Suffrage movement. In contrast to their views, a letter writer to the *Hastings Observer* stated that 'the position of those who would deny women the Parliamentary vote is that of a one-legged stool, it can't stand' and in an attack on the anti-suffragists, commented that 'those women who now try to prop it up will be the first to drop it, and rush to the polls when... justice struggles free of the entanglement of blind prejudice...'

Planning meetings

In January 1911 the Hastings and St Leonards Women's Suffrage Propaganda League met to plan the year's campaigning activities. WSPU member Helen Ogston and Cecil Chapman of the Men's League for Women's Suffrage were the main speakers. The view of the meeting was that the 'future of the movement depended on our determination over the next few months to get a Bill brought forward in the new Parliament.' Mrs Darent Harrison and Mrs MacMunn felt the future was hopeful because at least 400 MPs in the new Parliament were pledged to votes for women.

Over the next two or three months, campaigners discussed various options, which included tax resistance. Mrs Margaret Kineton Parkes, secretary of the Women's Tax Resistance League, addressed activists at a big meeting at the League's offices in London Road, promoting tax resistance and explaining the reasons why it was effective: 'one as a weapon, another as a protest and another as propaganda.' She said it might be a disagreeable thing to do but 'when we realise what other people have been willing to sacrifice to the movement, we ought not to begrudge a few pieces of furniture being sold up.' When the meeting finished, Isabella Darent Harrison expressed her intention to be a tax resister.

A Liberal government had been returned in January and Liberal MP George Kemp had put forward a second Conciliation Bill. The Bill was widely discussed at meetings and through the local press: anti-suffragists were vociferous in their view that women should not have the vote, describing suffragettes as 'violent unbalanced creatures' and continued to argue that their polls indicated women did not want the vote. Isabel Willis in a calm, well-written letter challenged their findings and stated that only 'well-balanced, clear-headed, practical' women would be able to lead and organise such a remarkable movement as the 'Women's Suffrage Movement.' The word 'violent' should be applied instead to 'describe the men whose recent exhibition of arm twisting, kicking and other kinds of torture' had led to some MPs calling for an official enquiry.

In February Janette Steer of the Actresses' Franchise League came to Hastings and spoke to a large meeting organised by the Women's Propaganda League. The *Hastings Observer* commented on the variety of badges worn by attendees, which gave visual evidence of the number of suffrage societies that had 'sprung into being during the last few years, all working in different ways for the same object.'

Boycotting the census

The second Conciliation Bill passed its first and second readings with a clear and healthy majority. However, only a few weeks later Lloyd George, Chancellor of the Exchequer announced the government could not give more time to the bill and that it would be shifted to the next parliamentary session, which opened in September 1911. In response the WSPU called for women householders to boycott the coming census, with the slogan 'No Vote, No Census'.

Mrs Darent Harrison, Mrs Edith Bowerman Chibnall, Mrs MacMunn, Miss Lettice MacMunn, Miss Willis, Miss Hogg, Miss Tristram and other local campaigners responded to the call and held a meeting to plan their strategy. Their aim was to avoid filling in the census forms; this meant leaving their homes and spending the night elsewhere. They could either hide or an activist would invite many women to spend the day and night at her house. The homeowner would then refuse to put her name on the form and also those of her friends.

On census day 2 April, the women put their plans into action. Mrs Darent Harrison stayed in her own house but invited suffrage friends to spend the night. Interviewed by the press the following day, she was in excellent spirits and laughed when she told the reporter that two or three plain clothes detectives, a police constable and an inspector had hovered around her house to spy on her guests. 'But they could not find out how many I had got, because they were coming and going, morning, afternoon and night.' Mrs Darent Harrison wrote 'no vote, no information' on her own census form but refused to include the names of her guests. She left instructions for her form to be given to the official when he called the following morning. The official asked to see Mrs Darent Harrison and read the official requirements to her, pointing out that she risked a £5 fine for not filling in the form. 'This he read with great emotion' said Mrs Darent Harrison and looked puzzled when she pointed out that she also risked one month's imprisonment. 'He forgot the month's imprisonment…he did not seem aware that there was a way out of paying £5, so I suggested the alternative and he fled in dismay.'

Nora MacMunn also took part in the census boycott and together with other passive resisters spent an uncomfortable night at 5 Grand Parade: 'It was cold so we had to light a stove, and the light from this could be seen outside… Presently we heard a rattling at the door, and a strong light flash in. We knew who it was because it was a very heavy tread, and unfortunately we were just getting very sleepy. The rattling…went on for some time but finally…all was peace…but in about ten minutes time there was suddenly a great noise above our heads. How anybody could get on the roof is a mystery, but we saw the light shine through the skylight although it didn't seem to produce anything…[and] the person on the roof…finally withdrew. This went on at intervals…but when we left…about half-past seven, the coast was quite clear.' Another local woman said when she told the official that she would not sign the form because she was a suffragette, 'He gave a most piteous sigh, and I felt quite nervous for his heart. He then gave one gasp, and left the room.'

The local activists were delighted with their actions and nationwide the census boycott was a great success. It made headline news. The *Hastings Observer* had no doubt that 'an instrument of the State has been nullified' and maybe with a slight note of pride, went on to say that 'perhaps few realised that Hastings Suffragettes were unusually to the fore in [the] campaign.' Clearly the local press was very interested in the event and the *Hastings Pictorial Advertiser* featured a large photograph of the 'Ladies who Evaded the Census' on its front page. It is a splendid photograph showing Mrs Darent Harrison and her co-tax resisters in

Isabella Darent Harrison and other women who evaded the census. *Hastings Pictorial Advertiser*

front of their banner, looking determined and dressed up to the nines in their Edwardian hats and fox furs.

Protests and the bill torpedoed

In May 1911 members of the Women's Suffrage Propaganda League travelled to London to present a petition to local MP Arthur du Cros urging him to support the Conciliation Bill. Most already knew the chances of his doing so were very slim. He stated publicly that he was opposed to women's suffrage in principle and could not support it 'unless it was clearly approved not only by a majority in the country itself. Therefore he would continue to vote against the Conciliation Bill.' Local suffrage societies continued to hold weekly meetings, which meant that at least three suffrage meetings took place every week in Hastings and St Leonards. There were also several public meetings. Lord and Lady Brassey attended a number of the public meetings, being prominent supporters of the NUWSS. It was noted at one meeting that the Conciliation Bill had passed its second reading by a large majority. Lady Brassey and her husband also held meetings at their London house in support of women's suffrage.

Sticking to her decision Mrs Darent Harrison had refused to pay her tax so, as a result, some of her goods, which had been taken by bailiffs, came up for sale as Lot 183 at the auction rooms in Norman Road. Making maximum use of a propaganda opportunity, Mrs Darent Harrison escorted by other women arrived at the auction rooms carrying banners emblazoned with the words 'No Vote, No Tax'. The noise of their arrival drowned the auctioneer who appealed to the women to leave, which of course they refused to do. Instead, led by Colonel Savile, they proceeded into the auction rooms. Colonel Savile protested the sale, and Mrs Darent Harrison's niece bought the goods. The procession, which now numbered around 50 people, then made its way from the auction room down Norman Road and Warrior Square to the seafront, up London Road and down Kings Road to the Concert Hall where a protest meeting took place.

In October Dorothy Bowker, an organiser with the WSPU, who had set up branches in various part of the country, arrived in Hastings to launch a local branch of the WSPU. She was not only responsible for Hastings but also St Leonards, Bexhill and Eastbourne. Soon afterwards, in November, the WSPU opened a shop at 8 Trinity Street, now Claremont. The shop sold the suffragette paper *Votes for Women* as well as WSPU badges and was the local WSPU headquarters. The shop was launched with an 'at home' event which Mrs Darent Harrison attended. Dorothy Bowker said that they still placed hope in the Conciliation Bill but stressed that if it did not pass, 'there would be war throughout this country as far as the women were concerned.' She urged women to 'bombard' du Cros saying 'Never let him feel for one second that there is not a strong body of women who will work against him in the next election if he does not alter his view.' Miss Bowker remained in Hastings for a few months then returned to London. Mary Allen, a well-known suffragette who been involved in window smashing, for which she had been imprisoned, embarked on a hunger strike and had endured force-feeding, replaced her as local organiser in February 1912.

Dorothy Bowker was realistic. A third Conciliation Bill had been introduced in September 1911 but in November to most people's amazement Asquith announced that he was introducing a Manhood Suffrage Bill, which might include women. Across the board suffragists and suffragettes were shocked and furious: in the words of Christabel Pankhurst Asquith had 'torpedoed' the Conciliation Bill. It limped on to a second reading in March 1912 but was doomed to failure. The Manhood Suffrage Bill also failed to get anywhere. At a stroke this effectively ended any real hope of achieving votes for women before the next general election, which was due to take place in 1915. However, what no one knew at that time was that there would not be an election in 1915 because the First World War would be underway.

A huge suffrage rally took place locally in November, organised by the Hastings, St Leonards and East Sussex Suffrage Society, now affiliated to the NUWSS. Millicent Fawcett spoke, as did Lord Lytton and other leading advocates of the non-militant suffrage societies. Mrs Fawcett said she thought it was a good sign that Asquith and Lloyd George had agreed to meet with a deputation of women but it was something of a false hope. The local Women's Propaganda League announced that it had now resumed its anti-Government policy and urged members to resist taxation until the vote was granted. They also passed a resolution: 'That the Committee of the Hastings and St Leonards Women's Suffrage Propaganda League protests against any extension of the franchise to non-taxpaying men until the claims of tax paying women have been satisfied and further calls the attention of the Government to the fact that whereas the women of this borough have conducted a vigorous campaign in favour of votes for qualified women extending over many years, not a single meeting has been called for the purpose of advocating manhood suffrage.' The resolution was sent to Asquith and Lloyd George.

Mrs Tubbs, Miss Jebb and Miss Young stand to the left, Millicent Fawcett and Miss Mosley to the right, at the big suffrage rally in the Public Hall, 15 Nov. 1911. *Hastings Pictorial Advertiser*

Waging war

Militancy escalated during 1912. With the Conciliation Bill torpedoed, the WSPU announced that the truce was over and some members embarked on a campaign of window smashing, setting fire to post boxes and occasional fire bombing.

The mood among the activists in Hastings and St Leonards also changed. There is a strong sense of anger and exasperation in the letters and meetings around this time, reflecting the frustration of women who had been campaigning for such a long time to get the vote and were constantly being betrayed by the Government. As one local woman said in at a meeting in January: 'They were no longer going to trust these men [Cabinet Ministers]. With them principle could go to the wall, so long as personal and party advantages did not.'

In the early part of the year the local WSPU and the Women's Propaganda League combined forces for a series of 'at homes' and meetings held either at the WSPU offices in Trinity Street or the Public Hall. Nora and Lettice MacMunn attended many of these meetings, as did Flora Tristram, Mrs Darent Harrison, Miss Willis and Mrs Isabel Giberne Sieveking. Mrs Sieveking, who was a cousin of the poet Gerard Manley Hopkins, grew up in Surrey and was herself an author. She arrived in Hastings in about 1909, lived in Exmouth Place, and soon joined the local WSPU and Mrs Darent Harrison's Propaganda League. Her letters appeared frequently in the *Hastings Observer*.

'May a "mere woman" correct a wrong impression... I was reported as having said that I longed to see "man equal to woman," and that I looked forward to the time when there would be no woman with wrongs unredressed. I have never looked forward to such a time, knowing well that while man is represented on this earth it is likely that I should have the longest "wait" ever recorded.'

Isabel Giberne Sieveking

Mrs Darent Harrison urged more women to become tax resisters and WSPU organiser Miss Bowker called for at least 20 local women to attend the next demonstration in London saying, 'We must have a great number of women in order that it is physically impossible to send them to prison.'

Weekly meetings at the WSPU Trinity Street headquarters were packed. A series of speakers arrived in Hastings, including

Beatrice Harradan, author and member of the Tax Resistance League, Alice Abadam, who asked her audience 'what in the name of common sense is the matter with English women that we are not allowed to vote?' and suffragette Jane Brailsford, who had served two prison sentences. In late January, at a very crowded meeting, Katherine Douglas Smith, a prominent militant declared, 'We have got to make ourselves so disagreeable that they cannot afford not only to ignore us but to ill treat us.' Barbara Ayrton Gould, daughter of mathematician Hertha Ayrton, gave a stirring address at the WSPU offices, saying 'It is now or never! We cannot afford to wait, and it means that women have got to come out and fight.' Soon after this Barbara Ayrton was one of 200 suffragettes arrested and imprisoned for breaking windows in London's Regent Street. In February 1912 when Mary Allen arrived as organiser, she enthralled her audience by describing her experiences in prison, on hunger strike and being force fed.

Suffragists broke new campaigning grounds in areas such as Silverhill, spreading the word further, and in March 1912 Mrs Darent Harrison, who was clearly becoming increasingly militant, Miss Bowker and others took part in a window smashing action in London. Miss Bowker was arrested; Miss Darent Harrison was not but she said she had no hesitation in saying the demonstration 'had done in half an hour what twenty years of constitutional propaganda has failed to do.'

By April Jane Strickland was well and truly running out of patience with the Liberal Party and sent a furious letter to the local press: 'Sixty-six Members who call themselves Liberals – that is, men who belong to the democratic party, whose motto is "no taxation without representation", voted against the Bill... An assembly of supposed intelligent and honourable men... stands condemned by its own deed as either dishonest or weak-kneed...unworthy of continued trust and confidence...' Interestingly she went on to state that the Labour party 'proved itself splendidly loyal to the women.' Not long after she said 'women will no longer submit to be fooled and betrayed by the [Liberal] Party,' and stated that she would put her future trust in the Labour Party.

Hastings suffragettes continued to hold meetings on the beach, either opposite what was then the Cinema du Luxe, now the amusement arcade, or opposite Warrior Square. Visiting speakers such as Elizabeth Billing, Jane Brailsford and Nora Dacre Fox, a particularly good public speaker, attracted large crowds of women and men. Local Conservative MP Arthur du Cros came in for a great deal of criticism. Isabella Harrison wrote to the press accusing him of betraying 'women householders of this borough' and four suffragettes heckled him with shouts of 'Votes for Women', when he arrived to speak at a meeting of the Primrose League. One of the four later wrote to the *Hastings Observer* saying they had been refused admittance to the Primrose League meeting and were followed by police wherever they walked. She wondered whether this might have been because each of them was carrying a walking stick. 'I expect it was the walking sticks which gave the Conservatives a bad attack of nerves. Perhaps the gallant police officers had visions of broken windows... Everybody seems to have been in a blue funk, and all the fear instilled in the Conservatives, the six constables, the one sergeant, the Superintendent, and three plain clothes officers, was because a few women had stood outside and dared to offer 'Votes for Women' to the gallant Borough Member.'

Weekly meetings continued to take place at the WSPU shop in Trinity Street. Elsie Bowerman chaired one of these in March, telling members that the movement had reached a critical point. She also read out a letter from a 'Hastings prisoner', namely Dorothy Bowker, who had set up the local branch originally and was then awaiting trial in for window smashing in London. She asked: 'Why are we shut out from the power of

'When women have gained
the Suffrage they will no
longer break windows in
order to obtain it.'
Isabel Willis

doing good. Is it a wonder that we come out and do desperate things in order to right these wrongs... it is as though we hear the voices of the children behind a door barred to us, a door we have to, and must, break down even if it means smashing plate-glass windows.'

Mrs Darent Harrison and co-tax resisters 'besieged' at 1 St Paul's Place. Courtesy of London Museum.

Under siege

Having once again refused to pay tax, in May 1912 Isabella Darent Harrison took a more militant stand, barricading herself into her house at 1 St Paul's Place and refusing to admit bailiffs. The outer doors of her house, which was 'smothered' in placards bearing political slogans, were locked and friends sent up food and other necessities in a basket on a rope. As Isabella Harrison pointed out, if the bailiffs really wanted to get in, they would have to break down the doors, so exposing them to the charges of criminal damage that suffragettes were experiencing.

The 'siege' lasted for just over a month. Bailiffs arrived with a so-called 'break open' warrant and started banging on the door. Mrs Harrison refused to open the doors, which were double locked and chained. 'For five or ten minutes nothing seems to have happened, until we heard a most ferocious bang, a fierce onslaught on the tradesmen's entrance. But they failed! It was doubly locked and chained... we heard them try another door in the basement... the noise was terrific.' Finally the bailiffs got in through a scullery window, only to find they were trapped in the kitchen, the door from the kitchen into the main part of the house also being locked. Eventually they seem to have picked the locks and made their way into the main part of the house, where they found Mrs Harrison who refused to speak to them 'I was not going to enter into friendly negotiation with the messengers of the King. I was militant through and through: it was war all along the line.'

The bailiffs seized a gold watch and some silver goods, which were due to be sold at auction subsequently. A protest, similar to the one that had taken place the previous year, was planned for the event. All suffrage societies were invited to attend. Miss Hogg of 36 Eversfield Place, a member of the WSPU and the Tax Resistance League, had also withheld tax and some of her goods had also been seized.

In June 1912 the local NUWSS opened a Women's Suffrage Club at 7 Havelock Road for more effective campaigning. The Club was a venue for meetings; it also had a 'rest' room where members could read or write and had a kitchen. Similarly the local WSPU moved its shop to larger premises at 8 Claremont. Commenting on these developments, Jane Strickland said, 'Let no one say that the Suffrage Movement in dead in this borough. On the contrary it was never so much alive.'

CHAPTER 6

Arson, bombs and riots

'The martyrdom of these women... will kindle a fire which
will not cease to burn until their cause is won.'
Mary Parr, St Leonards

The women's suffrage movement was most definitely still alive and it was becoming angrier. During 1912 militants and non-militants held increasing numbers of outdoor meetings. In London thousands attended meetings in Wimbledon, Ealing, Blackheath and Regents Park. In Hastings, large crowds arrived to listen to young women activists from the WSPU speaking about their personal experiences of arrest and force feeding and the need to fight the government. At the same time the Hastings and St Leonards Women's Propaganda League held its AGM at the Royal Concert Hall. By this time it had affiliated to another new suffrage society, the New Constitutional Society. It was announced that a branch of the Catholic Society for Women's Suffrage had also been formed. Mrs Sieveking, Isabel Willis, Miss Hogg and Miss Tristram resigned from the League's committee. Miss Smith, Miss MacMunn, Mrs Bonner and Miss Barber took their places. An 'at home' took place and the League's winter campaign was discussed. The local NUWSS branch also held various meetings at the Suffrage Club in Havelock Road. At one of the meetings in October 1912 Miss Maud Vickers spoke about the position of women in the sweated industries, matchbox makers, shirt makers, bonnet makers and so on, all of whom were on very low wages. Both she and indeed many other suffrage campaigners had no doubt that it was only by women gaining the vote that exploited women such as those in the sweated industries could be helped.

Letters

The number of letters sent to the *Hastings and St Leonards Observer* about the subject of votes for women increased dramatically and the battle lines between those in support and those against were clearly visible. As Isabel Willis wrote on 27 July 1913: '... the situation between the Government and the women has become ... strained and intense'. In her view the Government was totally responsible: 'In the days of the mildest militancy the harshest and most coercive methods were adopted in the effort to crush the movement, and in their dealing with the whole question, the Government has done nothing but resort to trickery and the breaking of faith and pledges. Adding to this the revival of forcible feeding, the temper of the women has become inflamed with resentment and indignation.' She reminded readers that Mrs Pankhurst had publicly stated that if the Government continued with 'its unstatesmanlike folly', the leaders of the movement would have difficulty in controlling the rank and file. Other local suffragists and suffragettes wrote to the press in much the same vein, deploring the actions of the Government and the horrors of force feeding, a dreadful procedure that involved prison staff holding down suffragettes, roughly inserting tubes into the woman's throat and pouring milk down the tube.

However not all members of the public were sympathetic. Mr AW Fluck of 43 St Helen's Crescent wrote that 'the half-witted creatures who go about breaking windows...are the very last people in the world to be entrusted with a Parliamentary vote.' In his view 'a more inglorious lot of females it is difficult to find.' When a staunch local male supporter, Mr Barclay Hanbury sent a long letter to the local paper describing the horrors of forcible feeding and quoting from eminent doctors such as Mr Charles Mansell-Moullin, a surgeon and also one of the founder members of the Men's League for Women's

Suffrage, who considered the procedure brutal and dangerous, a reply came back from Joseph F Green, who wrote that 'forcible feeding is 'doubtless extremely repulsive...but I would ask what is the Government to do...Had the Suffragettes been allowed to starve, the cry would be: "You are murderers"...'

Isabella Darent Harrison spoke for many local activists when she accused Arthur du Cros and 'all the Anti-Suffrage wire-pullers' behind him of 'double-dealing and thoroughly cowardly, unconstitutional, and dishonourable tactics' and urging him to pay what she described as a 'debt of honour to the women householders of the borough.'

> 'Women who demand the vote have been provoked and exasperated beyond endurance. They have been taunted and goaded by Cabinet Ministers and others into acts of violence.'
>
> **Isabella Darent Harrison**

Mrs Pankhurst speaks

Decorated motor cars and suffragettes with posters and sandwich boards saying 'Votes for Women' preceded the arrival of Mrs Emmeline Pankhurst, who arrived in Hastings to speak at a packed meeting at the Public Hall on Tuesday evening, 26 November 1912. Green and white flowers decorated the hall, which was full before the meeting began. Pretty well all the local suffragettes and suffragists were present, including Mary Allen of the WSPU, who had organised the meeting, Isabella Darent Harrison, Edith Bowerman Chibnall, her daughter Elsie Bowerman, Mrs MacMunn, Lettice MacMunn, Mrs Sieveking, Miss Tristram, Miss Hogg, and many others. There were also supporters from Bexhill, Brighton, Sedlescombe and Winchelsea. Also present were male supporters, many of them members of the local Men's League. Mrs Edith Mansell-Moullin spoke first saying they were meeting during ' a great crisis' in the history of the women's suffrage 'which demanded that

111

Poster parade, Eversfield Place, Hastings. *Hastings Pictorial Advertiser*

Standing, left to right: Emmeline Pankhurst, Edith Mansell-Moullin, Mary Allen at Suffrage Meeting, Public Hall, 26 November 1912. *Hastings Pictorial Advertiser*

Top: local suffragettes advertise the public meeting.
Below: Elsie Bowerman, seated in motor car outside WSPU local HQ, 8 Claremont
Hastings Pictorial Advertiser

those who had 'buckled on their armour... should turn a deaf
ear to everything else.' She believed that when the history of
this 'wonderful movement' came to be written it would be seen
that militancy was fully justified. She thought it was astounding
that activists could still believe that all that was required was to
continue 'peaceful propaganda work' and went on to say they
were fighting so that 'every girl should have a living wage, so
that she should not have to sell her body for bread.'

113

Mrs Pankhurst, described by the *Hastings Observer* as 'a slight figure dressed in black' then took the stage. As leader of the WSPU and a woman who had endured prison, hunger strikes and force feeding, Mrs Pankhurst commanded a great deal of respect from her audience. Her speech to the crowded hall was effectively a call to arms. She talked about her experiences as a poor law guardian in the North of England and how seeing poor women in workhouses and exploited factory women had contributed to her becoming a suffragette. She said that nothing would now make her believe that men would 'shield and protect women from all the dangers of life.' Knowing these things had made her a militant suffragette: people who had no constitutional rights could not hope to win the vote, or any other parliamentary reform, by constitutional means. For her, this was the whole basis of militancy. As far as she was concerned after fifty years of patient agitation for the vote, women were as much justified as men were from the time of Runnymede downwards to fight a civil war in order to win political liberty and constitutional rights. She went on to say, 'Property is the thing we have to attack, and even property we only attack very tentatively stage by stage. We won't be wasteful like men, who burnt out Bristol in a single night when they wanted the Reform Bill. We will begin very tentatively and always in faith that the moment will come when we reach the conscience and heats of men, and make them realise we have grievances.' She went on to say that there was more publicity in breaking a pane of glass than in ten thousand meetings; people often said that militancy put back the movement. 'Well,' she asked, 'How many of those women [at the meeting] would have gone to a Suffrage meeting six years ago?' She finished by saying that given the plight of girls and young women trafficked into what was then called the white slave trade, and in Salvation Army hostels, perhaps women 'had better break all the panes of glass in the world.'

Mrs Pankhurst then took a number of questions from the floor. Asked if militancy would continue if a Conservative government came in, she replied, to some laughter, 'We mean to get the vote from this Government, but if an accident happens to them...and the Conservatives came in, we should begin with them. We should ask very politely and nicely and if they were so foolish as their predecessors we should proceed to more drastic measures. I always say that after practising on the Liberal Government we should be quite perfect when we get to their successors.' After this she drove away.

Violent viragoes and sex war

In January 1913 Mrs Emmeline Pankhurst openly declared war on the Government. While not insisting on specific actions, she was nevertheless prepared to support any actions that were aimed at forcing the government to give votes for women. Over the next 18 months, militancy accelerated, reaching unprecedented levels as WSPU activists destroyed property, set fire to pillar boxes, embarked on large-scale window smashing campaigns, cut telegraph and telephone wires and attacked art treasures.

Unhappy with the increasing violence, some key figures broke with the WSPU, including Adele and Sylvia Pankhurst, who were effectively expelled, Emmeline Pethick-Lawrence, her husband Frederick and Beatrice Harradon who had spoken in Hastings, also left the WSPU. Others remained and an increasing number of young women were drawn into what was becoming for some of them, almost a spiritual crusade.

'The Suffrage agitation was a great spiritual warfare, the powers of darkness were opposing those of light, and although mistakes might be made, truth was great and would ultimately prevail'
Mrs Harlow Phibbs, Suffrage Club 1913

Campaigners in Hastings were as divided over militancy as anyone else but by and large even those long time law-abiding suffragists such as Mrs Jane Strickland, who did not agree with militancy, understood the reasons behind it. The general public was not impressed: the rather ferocious anti-suffragist who signed herself 'Annabel' wrote to the press decrying the actions of the 'militant Suffragettes', referring to their 'uncalled-for damages of property', setting fire to buildings, their 'wild onslaught on Parliamentary men, and bitter, unjust vituperation against men's attitude towards them... these violent viragoes seen to get intoxicated with political dram-drinking, and then act like maniacs.'

Naturally Isabel Willis responded immediately, refusing to take 'Annabel' seriously: 'To speak ... of the women who are engaged in the militant Suffragist movement as "violent viragoes, intoxicated with political dram drinking" is to provoke one to describe 'Annabel' herself as being "so inebriated with the exuberance of her own verbosity" as to be incapable of forming a sane judgement and therefore not to be taken seriously.'

By March 1913 Mrs Emmeline Pankhurst was under arrest again, Sylvia Pankhurst was in prison seriously ill and there was a public outcry when suffragette Lillian Lenton developed pleurisy as a result of food entering her lungs as she was force fed. As night follows day so events such as these were followed by a fresh burst of militancy. Jane Strickland put pen to paper and wrote to the local press: 'after each betrayal of the women's cause... militancy broke out afresh and with increased violence, until today we see it at the flood...this will become increasingly serious unless some way may be found out of the impasse...No punishment can kill the spirit of a movement based on a claim for justice and freedom...so it comes to pass that our statesmen are either callous or paralysed... Non-Militant Suffragists... ask, "What blocks the way to the granting of this demand?"... The answer comes back without hesitation, "The will of one man." Everyone knows that the so-called "loyalty to the Prime Minister" is at the root of the delay...Liberal Members break their pledge to the women ...The remedy for the crimes of the militant Suffragists is the removal of the injustice against which they fight.'

Given physical attacks on women, the brutality, imprisonments and force feeding, it is not surprising that some suffragettes came to see the continuing struggle as quite literally a sex war, with all men as the enemy. Christabel Pankhurst even adopted the slogan 'Votes for Women, Chastity for Men'. Activists were divided over this view, not least because it was an insult constantly hurled at campaigners whether militant or non-militant. Mrs Darent Harrison wrote to the local press rejecting the term 'sex war', saying 'Justice and freedom have no sex, and revolt against despotic government is a spiritual manifestation as sexless as in the case of... John Hampden [17th century parliamentarian and tax resister]... just as they had the support...of women, so we have on our side all the men who have realised how great is the injury that is done to nation by political subjection of the mother-half of the race...' Addressing a local meeting in the Lower Public Hall, Mrs Eugénie Bouvier, a WSPU member who spent time in prison, also denied that the women's meeting was a 'sex war', pointing out that more men were helping every day and that Hugh Franklin, of the Men's Political Union was in prison, while seven men had been arrested for protesting at a meeting where Lloyd George was speaking.

Cat and Mouse

In April 1913 with increasing numbers of imprisoned suffragettes going onto hunger strike and becoming dangerously ill, the Government introduced the Prisoners (Temporary Discharge for Ill-health) Act, known by activists as the Cat and Mouse Act.

It was an extremely cynical move, designed to prevent hunger-striking suffragettes from dying and therefore becoming martyrs. Under the terms of the Act suffragettes would be released early from prison if they were so weakened by hunger striking that they were at risk of death. Just as a cat plays with a mouse, so too the authorities would recall a suffragette to prison once her health was considered to have improved.

No matter what the general public thought of suffragettes, there was opposition to this Act. Protest meetings took place in Hastings and Jane Strickland wrote to the *Hastings Observer*, just before the Act was introduced saying 'Nothing short of a profound conviction that the present suffragist agitation is becoming a menace to society and a disgrace to the country, would justify me in asking you to allow me the use of your columns so frequently..' She also said that one of the reasons she was writing to the paper was because the London press were suppressing the facts, which is interesting and borne out by a number of local activists saying they thought the *Hastings Observer* presented a very balanced view.

Jane Strickland's letter was long and passionate; she outlined clearly the horrors of force feeding, quoted eminent physicians and church men who had denounced the practice and then went on to describe the Cat and Mouse Act: 'They [prisoners] are to rest in prison until within an ace of death, they are then to be hustled out, probably carried in a collapsed condition to the house of their friends, or to a nursing home, and then re-arrested, to undergo the same treatment again, if they violate the conditions under which they are licensed. And this in the Twentieth Century, in this England of ours! ... Mr McKenna admitted...that the spirit of these women is indomitable...yet, knowing that, he and his fellow Anti-Suffragists at Westminster are prepared, as they cannot break this spirit, to slowly torture the women to death, rather than to remove the cause of the militant outrages...'

Meetings and self-denial

Campaigners in Hastings and St Leonards continued with their weekly meetings. In April 1913 the Hastings, St Leonards and East Sussex branch of the NUWSS held its AGM at the Suffrage Club. Mrs Strickland presided and long-term members such as Mrs Harlow Phibbs, Miss Keyon, Miss Rance, who was the branch secretary and many others attended. Mrs Strickland commented that they had held 34 meetings over the last year, while the anti-suffragists had held only three: 'they appeared to go to sleep for three months, then wake up and hold a meeting, and afterwards go to sleep for another three months.' Clearly local activists had very little time or respect for the anti-suffragists

WSPU member Elsie Bowerman
Hastings Pictorial Advertiser

The local WSPU also organised a week of events in the Lower Public Hall, which attracted large and enthusiastic audiences. Mary Allan chaired the first event; she had recently returned from a two-month period in London working for the WSPU but was back with a wider remit; her responsibilities now including Folkestone and Dover. Other events included a talk by Miss Isabel Seymour who outlined the history of the WSPU, illustrating her talk with slides of processions, the inside of a prison cell, and a suffragette being force fed. There was also a talk on the White Slave Trade.

Then as now, campaigns needed money and a feature of local activity was the 'self-denial' week. As its name suggests members denied themselves something and gave the money saved to the cause. At one of the regular Monday meetings, Mary Allen commented that a Bexhill member had denied herself a hat in order to give 10 shillings to the WSPU.

Soon after the self-denial week, several local members, including Edith Bowerman Chibnall and Isabella Darent Harrison went up to London in April 1913 for a big meeting at the Albert Hall, where they presented £106 as a contribution from the Hastings district. Interestingly Edith and her daughter Elsie had not long returned to Hastings, after being in the United States. In April 1912 they had set sail for New York on the ill-fated Titanic and were fortunate to be among those who survived.

Levetleigh burns

In 1912 Christabel Pankhurst had made secret plans for an arson campaign, to be directed primarily against the houses of Cabinet Ministers and other known high-profile anti-Suffragists. Early attempts were unsuccessful but in February 1913 suffragettes successfully torched Lloyd George's country house in Surrey. Two months later the arson campaign reached Hastings when, on 15 April 1913, local Conservative MP Arthur du Cros' stately mansion Levetleigh in Dane Road, St Leonards went up in flames.

According to local reports, the first anyone knew of the fire was in the early hours of the morning around 1 or 2 am. Some reports said a policeman had spotted a light, another that neighbours had noticed flames. Either way the local Voluntary Fire Brigade soon arrived only to find the house was well alight. It appeared that fires had been started simultaneously in several rooms and not surprisingly they rapidly came to the conclusion that this was the work of suffragettes. Flames were bursting through the roof and the fire was not brought under control until about 5am. There were rumours that trails of paraffin paper stretched from one room to another and those early on the scene claimed to hear explosions. About 40 fire fighters were involved in putting the fire out. There was no loss of life, du Cros having moved out of the house three weeks earlier. The only person injured, according to press reports, was one of the firemen who fell into a prickly bush while pulling on a rope. The middle of the house and upstairs rooms were the most badly burned.

News of the fire spread quickly and by daylight quite a crowd had gathered. Investigators soon discovered that someone, presumably a suffragette or suffragettes, had got into the house via a small window on the ground floor, near to some bushes, which, according to the press, would have provided a hiding place. Traces of jam and brown paper being found, it was assumed that these had been used to cover the window before breaking it, to dampen any noise. Once through the window, access to the main part of the house was easy. Papers were found carrying the words 'Votes for women' and a postcard on which was written in capital letters: 'To stop militancy give votes for women.' These plus the fact that Arthur du Cros

Postcard found at Levetleigh after the fire. Right: broken window through which suffragettes entered the building. *Hastings Pictorial Advertiser*

was well known for his opposition to votes for women, made it pretty certain that suffragettes had carried out the attack. As the *Hastings Observer* concluded: 'That the Suffragettes owed Mr du Cros a grudge is easily conceivable, as he has consistently held decided views upon the question of Votes for Women, and has not failed to express them...Interviewed in London, Mr Arthur du Cros said he 'was not altogether unprepared for something of the sort.'

The Levetleigh 'outrage' as the *Hastings and St Leonards Observer* called it, made headline news locally. It was also reported in *The Times*, which emphasised that suffragist literature had been found at the scene. Local suffragists came under suspicion briefly though in fact Kitty Marion, an actress and prominent WSPU member was responsible. She lived in Harfield, Sussex and was a member of the Brighton WSPU. She also helped to set up the Actresses Franchise League. An advocate of direct action, she was arrested and went on hunger strike many times. During 1913 she was one of the leading activists in the arson campaign. Levetleigh was one of her many targets. It is included in the impressively long list of arson attacks itemised in *The Suffragette* of 26 December 1913.

Following the attack Mary Allen of the local WSPU branch was interviewed and told the paper that, as a militant society, they supported the action: 'we agree with any protest made to bring our question home to the Government unless that protest endangers life.' She and her colleague Miss Owen had visited the scene both openly wearing WSPU badges and she said there had been no demonstrations against them, although one or two people jeered at them. There was some slight damage to their premises the following night but rumours that the windows of the Suffrage Club had been smashed were untrue.

Hardly surprisingly there was a very strong reaction locally. Beth Finlay of the local anti-suffragist league described the arson attack as a 'wicked and dastardly deed' and 'criminal lunacy' and called on 'constitutionalists to condemn militants', asking 'what possible benefit can follow on the enfranchisement of women that would be commensurable with this degradation of our sex which militancy is bringing about.' Mr du Cros also joined in saying at public meeting of the local Conservative Party that women 'having failed to get the pledge they sought by fair means... now resorted to foul means...' He claimed that local suffragettes had known about the arson attack before it occurred and that 'those ladies had not only disgraced their sex but showed their absolute unfitness to be entrusted with any power.' He pledged to continue opposing votes for women – but of course this was nothing new.

However there were many campaigners who excused the action or pointed out the hypocrisy of the response. WSPU member Flora Tristram of St Leonards, who was very active in the local campaign, quoted a recent case where a man who had killed an 11-year old girl had received only one month's hard labour by which standard the punishment for the Levetleigh arson attack should be very short, unless 'property is of more value than the bodies and souls of women and girls.' Another response, this time from a man, Gordon Crosse, said that Miss Beth Finlay's protest might have more force had she ever protested the 'horrors of forcible feeding or the outrageous treatment to which women have been subjected... Miss Finlay cannot intend us to conclude that she considers Mr du Cros' house more valuable or more important than the bodies and souls of thousands of her fellow-women whose ruin she apparently contemplates without such "humiliation"...'

At a meeting at her house on 26 April, Mrs Darent Harrison said the burning of Levetleigh had brought votes for women directly into the forefront of public consciousness. People who had never done so before were now writing to the local press and she quoted Beth Finlay who had sent in a letter for the very first time, also Mr WV Crake, 'one of our most respected townsmen'. She had known him for years and he had never expressed any opinion on votes for women. Apparently indifferent to the fate of women imprisoned and undergoing severe sentences he was 'touched to the quick' at the thought of Levetleigh being burned. The meeting passed a resolution in support of tax resisters and protesting the 'cat and mouse' act. At the local WSPU meeting that week, Flora Tristram reported that copies of *The Suffragette* were selling so fast they had to order more copies.

Riots in Hastings

Until now local suffragists, whether militant or non-militant, had not experienced a great deal of hostility from local people. Christabel Pankhurst was the butt of some mob anger when she came to Hastings in 1908 but by and large the general public had confined itself to jeering, a few scuffles, throwing rotten fruit and a bit of heckling. This changed fairly dramatically during May 1913, probably because of Levetleigh.

On 6 May a riot occurred when Miss Billing from Bexhill came to speak at a WSPU open-air meeting in Wellington Square. The meeting began at 8pm by which time a large crowd of men, women and children had gathered. Standing on a chair, Miss Billing started speaking but was constantly interrupted. After about 20 minutes, members of the crowd rushed towards her. Clinging to a street lamp, and surrounded by a small band of supporters, including Mary Allen, Miss Hogg, Mrs Sieveking and some male supporters, she managed to continue until finally she was physically knocked off her chair. She was pulled to her feet and the crowd began jeering and booing as the 'little band of militants' made their way down Albert Road, closely followed by an angry crowd. Two male supporters had their hats pulled over their faces and were punched on the jaw; the women might also have experienced physical abuse had the police not finally arrived and escorted them along Queen's Road to the tram stop for Bexhill. Miss Billing then got onto a tram 'amidst a storm of hisses, mingled with applause.' The chair was smashed.

Just over a week later on 14 May there was a larger and much more aggressive anti-suffrage riot when angry and violent crowds attacked a procession of women protesting the sale of goods taken from local tax resisters. As before, Isabella Darent Harrison and her fellow tax resisters had planned a procession to coincide with the sale of their goods at the auction room and to highlight the injustice of taxation without representation. Margaret Kineton-Parkes, secretary of the Women's Tax Resistance League had come from London to join the procession, as had an American colleague, Mrs Percy Evans.

The procession was due to leave from Isabelle Darent Harrison's house and make its way to the auction rooms in Norman Road. Hostile crowds had already gathered before the march began and continued to attack the suffragettes as they made their way from Church Road, along the seafront and back to the Memorial. As the women bravely battled their way through a booing and jeering crowd, they were constantly attacked, their clothes torn and hats pulled off their heads. The crowd seized and destroyed banners and pelted the leading carriage containing Mrs Darent Harrison, Mrs Kineton Parkes and Mrs Percy Evans. As the procession made its way back to Norman Road, hostilities intensified as crowds rushed the suffragettes. Police unsuccessfully tried to hold back the crowds but a carriage was overturned near the auction rooms.

Women managed to get to safety but ugly scenes continued. An angry crowd gathered outside Mrs Darent Harrison's house and at the Concert Hall in Warrior Square where a suffrage meeting was due to take place that evening. Speakers and organisers, including Mrs Darent Harrison, Mrs Strickland, Cllr Reed and Miss Russell managed to force their way through

Scenes from the anti-suffragist riots, May 1913. *Hastings Pictorial Advertiser*

the crowds into the Hall, despite being rushed and pelted with flour. Much to Mrs Darent Harrison's annoyance, the authorities cancelled the meeting. Those inside were unable to leave because of the hostility of the crowds who remained at the entrance until about 10pm before slowly drifting away. Interviewed the next day, Isabella Darent Harrison was indignant, not least because *The Times* and other London daily papers had described the riot as a 'suffragette riot', when they should have called it an 'anti-

Torn banner and suffragists being taken to safety. *Hastings Pictorial Advertiser*

Broken windows, Green's Hotel in Havelock Road. *Hastings Pictorial Advertiser*

suffrage riot.' She also said that it was strange that people 'can be so stupid as to imagine that the women's cause can be crushed by methods which must be condemned by every respectable and intelligent Anti-Suffragist.'

However rioting had not yet run its course. On 20 May there were ugly scenes at a daytime open-air WSPU meeting in Wellington Square. Hundreds of people gathered in the Square where they heckled, threatened and jeered the speaker, Mrs Gough from London. When the crowds showed signs of rushing the speaker, the Mayor appealed for calm. After about half an hour, the police and the Mayor escorted Mrs Gough to the station, jeering crowds following them from Wellington Square.

That evening the Suffrage Club was attacked. According to the press, thousands of people had gathered in Wellington Square expecting another suffragette meeting. This did not happen so the crowds swarmed to the Suffrage Club in Havelock Road where one of the ordinary suffragist meetings was taking place. Mrs Ruth Kenyon, Jane Strickland and Mrs Raymond Pelly were inside as were many of the local suffragists. While they were speaking hostile crowds filled the streets around the Club and began pelting the Club's windows with flour. When the women tried to leave, they were assaulted and there were scuffles in the road leading to Priory Street. Police battled with the crowd, while women managed to get away. Ruth Kenyon got away in a motorcar, though crowds pelted it with eggs and flour and managed to smash one of the windows. One suffragist had her hat torn off and her purse stolen. Hearing a rumour that one suffragist was hiding in Green's Hotel at the top of Havelock Road, crowds surged to the hotel where they smashed some windows. Police were unable to disperse the crowds until about 11pm.

128

Bombs and police files

Feelings were clearly running very high in Hastings and there was panic about suffragette militancy, not least because suffragettes were bombing public buildings. Local police files record some anonymous bomb threats, including a written warning that the local police keep 'a sharp lookout on the Brassey Institute because 'it would be a great pity to see it burnt to the ground.'

Between 9 and 19 May three crudely made bombs were found and examined by the police. Documents about them are in a file labelled 'Militant Suffragettes 1913' at the East Sussex Records Office, The Keep, Sussex University. On 15 May the verger of the Holy Trinity Church, Trinity Street, found a large tin canister containing shavings, saltpetre, gunpowder and old rags that had been soaked in petrol plus two half bricks and a wax taper. A label 'Votes for Women, No Law, No order till we get the vote' was attached to the tin.

The following day another home made bomb was found on the staircase of the Brassey Institute. Mr Butterfield, the caretaker, found the tin, which was ticking. When opened it was found to contain a large stone, small clock and smouldering cigarette butts. No damage was done. Finally on 19 May a local tobacconist took a bomb-like article into the police station. It looked like a battery cell and had two copper wires attached.

It is very probable that in the feverish atmosphere these bombs were hoaxes, designed to cause panic rather than anything else. Certainly the local suffragettes denied all responsibility and Mrs Sieveking wrote to the local press saying that the local WSPU had absolutely nothing to do with the bomb placed in Holy Trinity Church.

Even so the local police continued to get tip-offs from members of the public. Mrs Grace Beaufort of 15 St George's Road contacted the police to say that she could hear machines running in the basement of 8 Claremont where the WSPU had its local headquarters. The police seem to have taken no action. A local bricklayer, Henry Prior of 2 South Terrace, Halton, brought in an anonymous letter written in capital letters that he had found on the pavement in Collier Road. It was handwritten, threatened revenge and supposedly came from the local Tax Resistance League, who of course knew absolutely nothing about it.

Interestingly though the files contain a pencilled letter from Laura Leighton, WSPU, Hastings from The Laurels. Addressed to 'Dear Charlotte', the letter says she has heard from Mrs Hammond who advises local WSPU members to smash windows in Robertson Street and to burn gorse on the East Hill. 'This information to be circulated among local WSPU members.' There is no record of these instructions being carried out.

By this time many of the WSPU leaders were in prison or in hiding and the WSPU was effectively operating as an underground organisation. The file contains an interesting booklet of photographs and biographical information on all the known militants. Sent out by the CID, the 'memorandum' was circulated to all police stations so that members of the local police force could keep an eye open for and would be able to recognize militants arriving in their town. Hastings police obviously received a copy of this 'memorandum', which is a comprehensive, very well produced and detailed document, indicating how well the police were gathering information. It contains photographs of all the known activists, including Mary Richardson, Flora Drummond and Kitty Marion and lists all their convictions and actions. Many of the women are described as 'extremely dangerous'. Kitty Marion, the Levetleigh arsonist, is described as 'capable of committing any outrage.'

The file also contains detailed correspondence between Mrs Kineton Parkes of the Tax Resistance League and the Chief

Constable of Hastings. The letters were written in July, referring back to the riot that had taken place in May against the tax resisters. Mrs Kineton Parkes and Mrs Darent Harrison were extremely clear that the riot had been orchestrated by a man called Mr Sparling and had been asking the Chief Constable to take action. Mrs Kineton Parkes mentions that she, Mrs Darent Harrison and others can provide witness statements and swear to the man's identity but as of July 1913 no action had been taken and no one was ever charged with assaulting the women.

The aftermath

Immediately after the riots a number of prominent activists including Jane Strickland, Isabella Darent Harrison, Miss Hogg, Miss Rance, Mrs MacMunn went to the police to register a complaint about the inadequacy of the police presence. Mrs Strickland was keen to stress she was not complaining about police behaviour but their numbers. Mrs Darent Harrison also wanted to make a complaint about Mr William Slade having effectively prohibited their public meeting by closing the Concert Hall. Veteran campaigner Mrs Tubbs, now vice-president of the local NUWSS, blamed the rioting on placards saying 'Dastardly Destruction of Levetleigh by Suffragists' which had been posted around town. She called on the Mayor to have these removed. She also reminded people that the Suffrage Club belonged to members of the NUWSS who were and always had been non-militant. Therefore, as she said, no members of their branch could or would have had anything to do with the arson attack on Levetleigh.

One of the first results of the riots was that a rescheduled tax resistance meeting at which Mrs Cecil Chapman, president of the New Constitutional Society, Mrs Kineton Parkes and Miss Margaret Douglas were due to speak, was cancelled. The syndicate that ran the Royal Concert Hall was not prepared to

'It was astounding that, in this Old Cinque town, whose sturdy population made such a gallant stand against the armed Normans, their descendants should now be guilty of felling defenceless women to the ground...'

Pro Bono Publico, St Leonards

risk damage to the hall. Similarly a suffragist meeting scheduled for mid June and due to be chaired by Earl Brassy was cancelled on the advice of the police.

Earl Brassey protested the riots and brutality towards the women, while Frederick Barclay Hanbury expressed his admiration in a letter to the press: 'They [the women] deserve nothing but honour and respect for the fortitude they showed throughout the terrific struggle... nothing daunted them, they marched on and on... My blood boiled with indignation to witness the insults... they endured... What is all this about? The women of Great Britain, Scotland and Ireland want to have equal opportunity with the men to voice their grievances with effect to the Parliamentary vote...'

Hanbury's question was a fair one. Why was there such a powerful and destructive reaction to women who were simply asking for fair representation? Not many local people seemed to have an answer. There is little doubt that the violence was very shocking and many people could hardly believe it had happened in Hastings. One letter writer commented that he personally knew of 'several visitors who are leaving...who said that they... would not return to a place where such brutal feelings prevailed...' Admittedly the letter writer was partisan and also expressed considerable admiration for the women – and for the socialist men who rushed to their defence.

Still campaigning

Towards the end of June Hastings suffragettes speaking on the Market Green in Battle were pelted with flour and rotten eggs. An angry crowd hurled fireworks and other objects at the women, shouting at them to go home. The women managed to make their escape and caught the train back to Hastings.

After this tempers seemed to calm down and the various local suffrage societies continued with their regular meetings and 'at homes', all of which were very well attended. In July Jane Strickland and Kate Rance joined and walked with the Kent section of the Women's Suffrage Pilgrimage, which had been organised by the non-militant NUWSS with the aim of demonstrating to the Government how many women wanted the vote. The pilgrimage was entirely peaceful, women setting off from different geographical regions around the British Isles: the northwest, north east, midlands, east, southeast and southwest. Some walked, some cycled and a few travelled by car. On 26 July 1913 an estimated 50,000 arrived in London's Hyde Park as the different pilgrimages converged in the capital city.

Campaigners also continued to flood the local press with passionate letters. Isabel Giberne Sieveking was one who wrote in some despair: 'The weeks drag out, and drag out, but no strong irresistible protest comes from the country to the Cat and Mouse Bill... here we are in the Twentieth Century allowing in our midst slow torture to women... We, who pride ourselves on our civilisation, are acting on the methods of medieval times... The spiritual signboard which shows everywhere... is clear for every woman: "No thoroughfare!" But... because there exist in our midst women who cannot rest while such terrible injustices and wrongs go on unchecked... as the White Slave Traffic, Sweated Labour, assaults upon unprotected women and little children... there should be framed a law to punish and torture these heroic Englishwomen who are doing their utmost to bring in reform and agitate for long delayed justice to be measured out to the poor and down trodden. Yet this is what we are doing as a nation today. We are doing nothing more nor less than giving our consent to legalised tyranny and injustice when we allow a Bill such as the Cat and Mouse Bill to torture and make life impossible to reformers.'

The ban on public meetings finally ended and in October 1913 a huge suffrage rally took place at the Royal Concert Hall. Speakers included the Earl of Lytton, Earl and Countess Brassey, and Margaret Ashton, who in 1908 had become the first woman elected to the Manchester City Council. A month later, the long postponed meeting of the Tax Resistance League finally took place. Speakers included Mrs Kineton Parkes and Laurence Housman, a socialist, pacifist and co-founder of the Men's League for Women's Suffrage. In November also, Mrs Darent Harrison and two of her fellow tax resisters won their case against the Mayor and Hastings Council for compensation for the cost of damages at Green's Hotel on the night of 20 May. The *Hastings and St Leonards Observer* covered the court case in great detail, noting that when the court found in favour of the tax resisters, there were cheers and cries of 'Votes for Women.'

Publicising the cause: Miss Hogg sits in the front of a car while Isabelle Willis sits at the back. Suffragist supporter, Rev. H K Hope lends his car for the occasion. *Hastings Pictorial Advertiser*

CHAPTER 7

The Vote Won

'The fifty years' struggle was over.'
Ray Strachey

The year 1914 opened with a rather clever poem in the *Hastings and St Leonards Observer*. Entitled 'A Suffragette's Farewell to the old Year, 1913' and signed KT, it caught the spirit of the previous year rather well:

Good-bye, Thirteen, unlucky fellow,
With age all shrivelled up and yellow!
No more shall you with baneful luck
At Suffrage women run amock.
Nor feed by force when you have caught her,
Nor let her hunger strike on water.
Your year of persecution done.
Triumphant leaves the unconquered one!

The local suffrage societies continued to meet regularly and to hold public meetings. The *Hastings Observer* commented that local suffragists were never at a loss to 'secure speakers of the first order' and on 5 February 1914 Muriel Matters returned to Hastings to speak at a meeting at the Palacette, formerly the Pelham Hall Assembly Rooms, and from 1909 site of Hastings' first full time cinema. The local NUWSS organised the meeting. Muriel Matters called on the government to introduce a women's suffrage bill and commented there might be some who imagined their movement was one of 'shrieking women' out for votes because they could not get husbands. However no one who saw one of the great processions going through London could possibly imagine that and anyway in her view, 'the vote would be of more use to them at present than husbands.'

Three days later on Sunday 8 February the congregation of St Mary Magdalen Church was startled when a dozen local suffragettes staged a protest, repeating a special prayer 'O God, save Rachel Peace and Kitty Marion and all those who are persecuted and suffer for conscience sake and make our Bishops and Clergy see the justice of their cause...' St Mary Magdalen and various other churches had agreed to include the prayer, but it came as something of a surprise to the congregation. Suffragettes stood up while the prayer was recited and handed out leaflets afterwards.

By March 1914 Flora Tristram had taken over as chair of the local WSPU. The local branch, while remaining women-only, welcomed the fact that the local men were forming a branch of the Men's Political Union in Hastings and St Leonards. The local WSPU continued to flourish: in April 1914 Flora Tristram announced to a meeting at the Metropole in Robertson Terrace that sales of *The Suffragette* had 'gone on splendidly' and that their funds were in an excellent state. By contrast, on a national level the WSPU was floundering. Militancy continued but membership was declining significantly. Police restrictions on the Union's activities and constant raids on the London offices had seriously damaged the WSPU. Funds were seized and public venues closed to their meetings. By 1914 many militants were in poor health due to repeated imprisonments and hunger striking. Others, including the leadership, had virtually gone underground. Christabel Pankhurst, for instance, was in Paris.

The constitutional or non-militant societies in Hastings and St Leonards also continued with their campaigning, believing that eventually the government would be forced to introduce a woman's suffrage reform bill. As with the WSPU, members of the non-militant societies from the Woman's Propaganda League through to the local NUWSS increasingly spoke about the conditions of women in the sweated trades. Membership of the various local suffrage societies was always predominantly middle-class with a smattering of highly privileged women but it is clear that involvement in the suffrage campaign increased middle-class women's awareness of their more oppressed sisters. Some were even beginning to question the basis of imperialism and to raise concerns about women in other countries. For instance, in 1912 when local suffragists had taken meetings further afield to Silverhill, the speaker on that occasion, Mrs Pertwee, had stated that unlike men, suffragists, when considering imperialism, did not just see the government of India but 'cared about the condition of every single individual of the Empire, even the poorest infant in the slums.'

'Even more imperatively now than in times of peace do their members feel the need of enfranchisement, when so much depends upon the action and the help of women.'

Nora MacMunn

War changes everything

The outbreak of the First World War in August 1914 changed everything. With the arrival of a war the like of which had never seen before, the question of women's suffrage was effectively put on the back burner.

Reflecting what was happening at the national level, the local NUWSS almost immediately announced it was suspending political work and offered the services of its members to 'relieving the national distress.' Within days Jane Strickland had effectively turned the Suffrage Club into an 'aid bureau' for those suffering as a result of the war, including refugees and foreign-born residents. Writing to the local press she said: 'Suffragists feel bound to face their responsibilities, as members of a world-wide movement, to support every effort to restore peace and establish a wider Entente between all nations.' On 29 August they announced, via a front page advertisement in the local press, that members of the Suffrage Club were organising as an Emergency Corps, preparing to: investigate cases of distress among foreign women or girls in the borough; provide emergency beds; keep a record of available homes or rooms for refugees or war wounded, and to supply interpreters for a variety of languages, including French, German and Esperanto. By September they had announced that the newly formed Women's Emergency Corp of the NUWSS would be holding a meeting at the Suffrage Club in Havelock Road.

To start with not all suffrage societies followed suit. Nora MacMunn wrote to the paper in early September to say that many suffrage societies would continue to do their work of 'keeping before the public and the Government the necessity, especially apparent at this time, when a united effort of a whole free people is just what the country needs, of rendering a tardy justice to women and giving them their rightful position as free and responsible citizens.' She pointed out that the United Suffragists, a large and influential body, the Women's Freedom League, the East Federation of Suffragettes, the Cymru Suffrage League, Irish Women's League, the Church League for Women's Suffrage, and the Hastings and St Leonards Propaganda League, would be doing relief and emergency work but would also be keeping up their suffrage propaganda activities.

> 'Let us show ourselves worthy of citizenship, whether our claim to it be recognised or not.'
> **Millicent Fawcett**

In December Isabella Darent Harrison, sticking to her guns, wrote to the local press in on behalf of the local Women's Suffrage Propaganda League, protesting against compulsory registration on the National Register for war work without giving women the vote: 'We know that our country needs us for many forms of national service, and it is this knowledge which imposes upon us the duty of demanding that we shall be placed in a position to serve as free women, and not as docile and irresponsible tools. Unless the Government sees its way to pass an Emergency Bill conferring on women householders all the rights and responsibilities of citizenship… they… have no right to lecture us as to what is or what is not our duty in this hour of national danger…' With the country at war her view was not only unpopular it was also roundly condemned as unpatriotic by members of the general public and the *Hastings Observer*.

The WSPU suspended suffrage activities and to many people's surprise, having waged war so ferociously against the government for so many years, called a truce and threw its support firmly behind the government. Mrs Pankhurst demanded the right of women to serve and was a major recruiting figure throughout the war. Many suffragettes also took part in the rather shocking white feather campaign.

In November 1914 Flora Tristram wrote to the local press, stating that 'the Hastings and St Leonards branch of the Union is most keen to join in all Municipal schemes started for bringing the War to a swift and victorious conclusion, or for helping the wounded and distressed in the borough.' She also sent in extracts from Emmeline Pankhurst's recent speech in which, among other things, Mrs Pankhurst had said, 'It is perfectly true that until this War broke out we were engaged in a civil war, the purpose of which was to win from a reluctant Government the citizenship of the women of this land. But never throughout the whole of that fight did we for one single moment forget the love we had for our country…it was because we love our country so much that we could not bear to be the serf sex.'

As time went on and once it became obvious that this war would not be over by Christmas, increasing numbers of suffrage societies dropped political work completely to focus on the war effort.

The war years

The story of women's work and lives during the First World War is fascinating, complex and too detailed to be covered fully here, so what follows is a brief glimpse. The received image is that all women threw themselves patriotically into war work, and indeed most did so. Generally women did whatever they could to support the war effort, even if some had reservations. During the war years women entered and undertook a whole range of occupations, often taking up work previously done only by men and which, in peacetime, would have been considered highly unsuitable for women. As growing numbers of men were poured into the trenches, women workers were needed to replace them and from 1915 women were actively mobilised for work. As a result women became increasingly visible as drivers, clerks, painters, welders, policewomen and transport workers. They donned trousers to work on the land, drove buses, trams and motorcycles, acquired carpentry and engineering skills, built aircraft, worked in construction and entered the munitions factories in droves. Hundreds of women were recruited as typists, clerks and coders for the newly created British Intelligence service, as well as taking up work in banks and post offices.

Middle-class women who had been involved in suffrage campaigning had acquired excellent organisational and other skills, which they put to use setting up committees and societies to help refugees, trace missing servicemen, and assist unemployed women. They were excellent fundraisers, set up soup kitchens, ran flag days and worked in recruitment. Women also treated the wounded as doctors and nurses in Britain, France, Serbia and other war-torn countries. Initially the British government was slow to accept help from highly qualified women surgeons and doctors who, as a result and acting on their own initiative, set up women's hospitals and medical units in Belgium, France, Serbia and Russia. Women also worked as nursing orderlies and ambulance drivers, one of the best known and perhaps flamboyant group of women being the First-Aid Nursing Yeomanry (FANYs), who worked directly on the front line driving ambulances and helping the wounded. Middle-class women also entered the police force and worked as factory inspectors, overseeing and checking on conditions for the thousands of working-class women who poured into the munitions factories. And from 1917, women were finally recruited into the forces, entering the Women's Army Auxiliary Corps (WAAC), the Women's Royal Naval Service (WRNS) and the Women's Royal Air Force (WRAF), which was set up in 1918. Women were not allowed into combat but wore uniforms, learned to drill and carried out a range of support duties.

However, the arrival of war split the women's movement. While most suffragists and suffragettes supported the war, there were many who did not, including Sylvia Pankhurst and Muriel Matters. In fact most members of the Women's Freedom League (WFL) were pacifists. Some women campaigned for a speedy resolution to the war. They included former leaders of suffrage organisations such as Emmeline Pethick-Lawrence and Emily Hobhouse, who together with women's rights activists from around the world set up the International Congress of Women at the Hague in 1915, otherwise known as the Women's Peace Conference. More than 1,200 women from 12 different countries met at The Hague to try and find a way to end the war. Delegates from the conference met with various statesmen to lobby for peace but without success. One lasting achievement was however the creation of the Women's International League for Peace and Freedom (WILPF), still active today. Other women, risking imprisonment and social ostracism, actively supported conscientious objectors, the men who refused to fight on grounds of conscience. A number of former suffrage campaigners, well experienced in organising and also dodging the police, put these skills to good use keeping the No-Conscription Fellowship going when the men were imprisoned and continuing to produce its newspaper *The Tribunal* throughout the war years.

The vote won

In 1918 women's long fight for the vote achieved a major victory. After more than fifty years of continuous struggle – in fact fifty-two years after Barbara Bodichon's petition – the Representation of the People's Act finally enfranchised women over the age of 30 who had the necessary property qualification, including married women. The same act abolished property and other restrictions for men and extended the male vote to all men over the age of 21.

Moves towards extending the vote had begun in 1916, even with the country at war. Under the electoral system as it had existed since 1884 a large percentage of the male population was still without a vote and it was clear that with so many thousands of men fighting and dying for their country, men without a vote needed to be enfranchised. In December 1916 Lloyd George became Prime Minister. Unlike Asquith, he was not a cast iron anti-suffragist and he realised that if the vote was to be extended to all men, women could no longer be excluded, particularly given that they were such an essential part of the war effort.

As a result a Representation of the People Bill was drawn up that enfranchised all men over the age of 21 and enfranchised a limited number of women, subject to age and property restrictions. Sylvia Pankhurst and her Workers' Suffrage Federation strongly opposed the terms of the bill, which clearly would not enfranchise working-class women and would maintain electoral inequality. However most women's suffrage societies, while recognising its failings, supported and welcomed the Bill with enthusiasm.

142

In March 1917 the *Hastings and St Leonards Observer* published a letter from Isabella Darent Harrison, enclosing a resolution that had been signed by representatives of various women's suffrage societies and many of the important women's professional and industrial organisations. The resolution stated: 'That we, representing the undersigned Societies, recognising that a Bill based on the recommendations of the Speaker's Conference will confer the suffrage upon women, though not upon the terms for which we stand, urge the Government to introduce such a Bill without delay, provided that it contains as an integral part provisions for the enfranchisement of women. The signatories are representatives of twenty-eight Suffrage Societies and Women's Leagues, including Mrs I.E. Harrison for the Hastings and St Leonards Women's Suffrage Propaganda League, and Mrs Jane E. Strickland for the Free Church League for Women's Suffrage.' The resolution was to be sent to all MPs.

'The greatest reform bill ever passed in any country.'

Isabella Darent Harrison

The Bill passed through both the Commons and the Lords and became law on 6 February 1918. The Act was a victory and enfranchised around 8.5 million women. However, it was a partial victory. Only around 40 per cent of the female population gained the vote. Notably absent were the working-class women who had worked in munitions and other wartime factories. At a women's meeting in Hastings in June, feminist and former NUWSS secretary, Ray Strachey talked about some of the failings of the Act, arguing that one of the reasons for restricting the woman's vote was that if all women had gained the vote they would have swamped male voters, not least because of the terrible losses of the First World War. Whether or not this was the reason for continuing inequality, campaigners such as Isabella Darent Harrison and many others saw the Act as a great achievement after what had been a long, hard and often bitter struggle.

On 9 February the *Hastings and St Leonards Observer* printed a glowing article under the banner headline: 'Women Get the Vote: At Last'. The article applauded the achievement stating that 'after more than half a century of strenuous work and almost unparalleled vicissitudes' some six millions of women had been at last enfranchised. According to the paper, scenes in the lobbies when Bill passed the Lords were 'enthusiastic to a degree' and when Mrs Fawcett appeared, she was greeted with 'exclamations of profound joy.' The paper went on to give a brief resumé of the women's suffrage activity in Hastings over the years, singling out some of the main campaigners, and urging enfranchised women not to forget 'that there yet remains some millions of their sisters still unenfranchised.'

In April 1918 the Women's Propaganda League, while recognising that more work was needed to gain full electoral equality, formally disbanded. Both Isabella Darent Harrison and Nora MacMunn felt they had achieved their aims but urged members to get involved with other suffrage societies still engaged in the fight. The local WFL branch continued to meet for many years. The Hastings and St Leonards Suffrage Society held some meetings but finally disbanded in 1919, handing over its premises – and furniture – to the local branch of the National Women Citizen's Association, which had been formed once it became clear that women were about to gain the vote.

Seven months later in November 1918 the Parliament (Qualification of Women) Act extended women's political involvement further by making it legal for women to stand for election to Parliament, something that anti-suffragists such as Mr WHB of 15 Wellington Place, Hastings, had been terrified of back in the 1890s. Commenting on the development the *Hastings Observer* said that while the London press had used words such as 'startling' and 'extraordinary' to describe this development, the *Observer* felt it was only a logical sequence to the 'far greater revolution which took place when the women were given the vote.' As far as the editors were concerned: 'if the war work of the women of Great Britain is a good guide, we can look forward with no misgivings to their appearance on the floor of the House of Commons.' Indeed the *Observer* 'confidently' expected that the entry of women 'into the life of Parliament' would result in long overdue reforms in housing, better conditions for workers and 'even an improvement in the tone and quality of Parliamentary debates.' The paper concluded by saying 'we have always been supporters of what is called the women's cause', which strictly speaking had not been the case in the 1870s. It is interesting to read that the *Observer*, as did many other commentators, frequently referred to women being 'given' the vote rather than winning or achieving it.

Women go to the polls

The general election of December 1918 was the first after the war and the first in which women could finally cast a vote. Across the country seventeen women stood for election, including Ray Strachey, who stood unsuccessfully as an Independent, Christabel Pankhurst, who stood for the short-lived Women's Party, which Christabel and her mother had formed in 1917, after the WSPU was dissolved. She stood in Smethwick and was narrowly defeated by the Labour Party's male candidate. Three members of the Women's Freedom League also stood – Charlotte Despard, Elizabeth How-Martyn and Emily Phipps. They stood in London boroughs but their anti-war views were unpopular and they were defeated. The only woman of the seventeen candidates to be elected was Countess Markievicz. As an Irish Republican though, she refused to take the oath of allegiance to Britain and the royal family, so did not take her seat in the House of Commons. It was not until the following year, in a by-election, that Viscountess Nancy Astor became the very first woman to be elected to the House of Commons.

Hastings and St Leonards did not post a woman candidate but in the run up to the 1918 election local women were very active. A local Women Citizens' Association was formed, one of many such local Associations and part of a national initiative, the aim of which was to stimulate women's interest in politics and prepare women for active citizenship. Lady Brassey was chair of the new Association; members included Mrs Ebden, Cecilia Tubbs and Ruth Kenyon, both of whom had a long involvement with the suffrage campaign. At its inaugural meeting in June 1918 Lady Brassey, dressed in VAD uniform, addressed a large and enthusiastic meeting, saying that now women had the vote it was their duty to study public questions and use the vote 'to the best advantage.' Ray Strachey spoke next on the subject of 'The Vote: Women's Responsibilities.' She said she would do her best to explain the new Act, which she described as a 'fair tangle of confusion' and pointed out various anomalies, for instance if three sisters lived together in a house only two would have votes, unless the third was a bonafide lodger, with her own furniture in her own room. She concluded by urging those women qualified to vote to register and commented that they had come into the 'political machine' just in time to help with the great work of post-war reconstruction.

In December the local group invited both parliamentary candidates, Mr JG Butler for Labour and Mr Laurance Lyon, the Coalition candidate, to attend one of their meetings to present their views and answer questions. The Women's Freedom League met on 9 December in Hastings Town Hall. Jane Strickland chaired the meeting and in her opening statement referred to the 'long and fierce struggle' women had gone through to achieve the vote and how neither political party had taken their case seriously. Now women had the vote, in her view the things to be aimed at were 'internationalism, absolute sex equality and freedom for women in every industry and sphere of life.' She was followed by Miss Underwood who gave an 'excellent' address on 'Why we need Women MPs in the next House of Commons.'

On the eve of the election the Hastings and St Leonards Women Citizens' Association and Kate Rance and Miss Underdown on behalf of the Hastings, St Leonards and East Sussex Women's Suffrage Society presented both candidates with a series of detailed questions to establish their views on a number of important issues, including whether or not they supported the extension of voting rights to women so that women and men should have equal voting rights, and their views on equal pay for equal work. The questions and answers were printed in the *Hastings Observer*.

On polling day itself, local women turned out in great numbers to cast their votes, despite dreadful weather. The *Hastings Observer* commented extensively on women's participation, saying that 'women voted extraordinarily well in all wards and quite disapproved the idea that they would not take sufficient interest to vote.' The *Observer* believed the oldest voter on the day was a Miss Osborne of Caroline Place, aged 94 and 'a wonderfully active old lady' and referred to a 90-year-old woman resident of Bohemia, who did not vote until late in the evening, having waited all day for a lift to the polling station. The paper also noted the 'interest shown by women who came to the poll in good numbers' and commented that in some wards women voters easily outnumbered men.

When the votes were counted, Laurance Lyon had won the seat comfortably, defeating the Labour candidate by a sizeable majority. One of Lyon's persuasive arguments had been that it was the Coalition government that had given women the vote.

Standing for parliament

The first woman to stand as a parliamentary candidate in Hastings was Maria Gordon, a geologist and women's rights

147

activist who stood unsuccessfully as a Liberal candidate in 1923. The following year Muriel Matters, who had visited Hastings so often, stood as a Labour candidate, one of only 27 women candidates countrywide. The *Hastings Observer* covered her election campaign fairly extensively, referring to her 'vigorous campaign' and commenting that 'Small though the chances of a Labour candidate in Hastings may be, Mrs Muriel Matters Porter and her supporters will lose no votes for lack of energetic campaigning. Meetings have been held every night this week, and large audiences have been addressed by the candidate, whose charm of manner captivates even those who are a little bewildered by her visionary and idealistic political philosophy. Her wide experience of other lands, her experience in the feminist movement and in education, and her reminiscences of famous men and women attract many who would be the last to support the Labour Party.'

Interestingly Muriel Matters launched her campaign in Ore on a Monday evening at the Ore Village School. Stalwart campaigner Jane Strickland, who by now was a Labour supporter, introduced the candidate describing her as 'a very old friend' and went on to tell the famous story of how Muriel Matters had chained herself to the grille of the Ladies Gallery in the House of Commons.

Muriel Matters was defeated and did not stand again. She and her husband, William Porter, lived in Hastings during the election campaign but it was not until 1949 when she was aged 72 that she finally settled in Hastings, moving into 7 Pelham Crescent. She remained in the town until her death in 1969, aged 92. She is remembered locally with a blue plaque, and a room in St Mary's in the Castle named after her. On 1 January 2017 the local council offices were renamed Muriel Matters House in her honour.

Hastings did not return a woman MP to the House of Commons until 1992, by which time the constituency included part of Rye. The first woman MP to represent Hastings and Rye was Conservative Jacqui Lait. She held the seat until 1997 when Michael Foster, Hastings' first Labour MP, defeated her. In 2010 Conservative Amber Rudd became Hastings and Rye's second female MP.

Local councillors

Hastings elected women as local councillors many years before the town chose a woman MP. In April 1919 Annie Lile and Ruth Kenyon stood as independent candidates for Hastings Borough Council. Backed by the Hastings and St Leonards Women Citizens' Association, the women argued that it was imperative that women should be on the council because so much of the council's work was concerned with matters that affected women, such as public health, housing, maternity and child welfare. In November 1919 Annie Lile, of 13 Pevensey Road, St Leonards, was duly elected, so becoming Hastings' first woman councillor. However, and despite all the developments in women's rights that have occurred since then, in 2017 out of 32 borough councillors in Hastings only seven were women.

Equal voting rights

On 2 July 1928, ten years after the first women gained the parliamentary vote, the Equal Franchise Act enfranchised women over the age of 21, finally enabling women to vote on the same terms as men. At a meeting of the Women's Freedom League later in July, Miss Underwood secretary of the local WLF said the Bill had received the Royal Assent so quietly that it passed almost unnoticed but the Women's Freedom League 'rejoiced', as did many other campaigners both in Hastings and elsewhere.

Some local campaigners were still around to see their hard-won goal achieved. They included tireless campaigner, Jane

Elizabeth Strickland, who went on to become vice chair of the local Labour Party until her death in 1932. Isabella Darent Harrison also saw both the 1918 and 1928 victories; she continued to live at 1 St Paul's Place until her death in 1943. Elsie Bowerman and her mother Edith were also able to celebrate both victories. Elsie went on to become the first woman barrister at the Old Bailey and helped to set up the UN Commission on the Status of Women in the United States in 1947. She kept a flat in St Leonards until Edith died in 1953. Elsie died in 1973 and like her campaigning colleagues is also buried in Hastings Cemetery. In 2005 thanks to the efforts of local historian Helena Wojtczak a plaque to Elsie Bowerman was unveiled at her home at 23 Silchester Road.

Other local campaigners did not live to see the final victory. Barbara Bodichon, who had been instrumental in kicking the whole campaign off with her 1866 petition, had died at her home in Scalands in 1891. Elizabeth Eiloart, one of the early activists died in Brighton in 1898. Novelist and suffragist Matilda Betham Edwards, friend of Elizabeth Fricker Hall, saw the 1918 victory but died the following year, while Isabel Hogg, known locally as the suffragette who sold suffrage papers at the Memorial, died in 1918, mourned by her close companion Flora Tristram. Veteran campaigner Fanny Cecilia Tubbs celebrated women gaining the vote in 1918 but died in 1922, six years before the final victory. Mrs Tubbs, Isabella Darent Harrison, Jane Strickland and Elsie Bowerman are all buried in Hastings Cemetery.

Eight years after the Equal Franchise Act, in August 1936, Sub-Inspector Frederick Turner retired from the Hastings police force after 26 years of loyal service. The *Hastings Observer* interviewed him and perhaps not surprisingly some of his most vivid memories were of previous elections and suffragette activity in particular: 'In the suffragette period there were many stormy incidents. I still remember escorting a procession while boulders were flying, and saw a Suffragette ducked in the old horse trough at the bottom of Warrior Square.' As the *Observer* commented, Turner's reminiscences might well lead readers to think that 'them were the days' – and so to some extent perhaps they were.

Starting from small beginnings in the late 1860s through to the turbulent years before the First World War, bands of thoughtful, determined women in Hastings and St Leonards devoted many years of their lives to the cause of achieving votes for women. They hosted meetings, booked public halls, took up public speaking, networked, wrote letters, lobbied politicians, joined huge marches, and even broke the law in their absolute commitment to winning the vote. Women living in Hastings and St Leonards today owe these dedicated campaigners a great deal.

BIBLIOGRAPHY

Books

Emmeline Pankhurst: A Biography, Jane Purvis (Routledge, 2002)

Eve and the New Jerusalem: Socialism and Feminism in the Nineteenth Century, Barbara Taylor (Virago, 1983)

Feminism: A Very Short Introduction, Margaret Walters (OUP, 2005)

Independent Women: Work and Community for Single Women, Martha Vicinus (Virago, 1985)

Miss Muriel Matters, Robert Wainwright (Allen & Unwin, 2017)

Notable Sussex Women, Helena Wojtczak (The Hastings Press, 2008)

The British Women's Suffrage Campaign 1866-1928, Harold L. Smith (Routledge, 2nd edition, 2007)

The Cause: A Short History of the Women's Movement in Great Britain, Ray Strachey (Virago, 1978, first published 1928)

Votes for Women, Paula Bartley (Hodder Education, 2007)

Women in Public: The Women's Movement 1850-1900, Patricia Hollis (George Allen & Unwin, 1979)

Women's Suffrage: A Short History of a Great Movement, Millicent Fawcett (first published 1912, available online: http://www.gutenberg.org/files/48614/48614-h/48614-h.htm)

Journals/periodicals

Hastings and St Leonards Observer: 1867–1914

The Hastings Pictorial Advertiser

The Times digital archive

Websites

https://www.britishnewspaperarchive.co.uk

http://www.hastingspress.co.uk/history/historyindex.html

https://www.parliament.uk/about/living-heritage/
transformingsociety/electionsvoting/womenvote/overview/
petitions/

https://www.parliament.uk/business/committees/committees-a-z/
commons-select/petitions-committee/petition-of-the-month/
votes-for-women-the-1866-suffrage-petition/

INDEX